Red Leaves

Jacqueline L. Smith

This book is a work of fiction. Any resemblance to actual events or persons, living or dead, is entirely coincidental.

"Red Leaves," by Jacqueline L. Smith. ISBN 978-1-62137-300-1.

Published 2013 by Virtualbookworm.com Publishing Inc., P.O. Box 9949, College Station, TX 77842, US. ©2013, Jacqueline L. Smith. All rights reserved. No part of this publication may be reproduced, stored in a retrieval system, or transmitted in any form or by any means, electronic, mechanical, recording or otherwise, without the prior written permission of Jacqueline L. Smith.

Manufactured in the United States of America.

From the Author

In today's society, men and women always share stories of happiness and sadness about falling in and out of love with someone. I wanted to share common relationship issues men and women face when dating, being in a long-term relationship, or being married. The goal for most people is to be content and happy with someone, but every now and then, a person will fall in love and the pain of ending the relationship is unexpected. Many relationships may not last when hoping to meet Mr. or Miss. Right. It's becoming common to want to be with someone who has the qualities to make a relationship work. Most do hope that a loving relationship will last, but because of the unexpected, many men and women are left in the dark about what is next, especially after being with someone intimately. Therefore, the search continues for many people.

Contents

A Man May Choose to Stay or Leave ... 1

A Ray of Sunshine ... 2

Accepting Whatever Goes ... 4

Always Expecting Material Things ... 5

Always Nonchalant ... 6

What Impresses You? ... 7

Are You Ready for the Chase? ... 8

Breaking Up Isn't Easy ... 9

Business or Pleasure Trips ... 10

Charlotte's Unfair Financial Situation ... 13

Cheating Debate ... 15

Couple's Private Bedroom Conversations ... 16

Crystal Tried to Move on From Kirk ... 17

Daphne's Love for Eric ... 19

Darrel's Forbidden Entry and Exit ... 22

Denise Said He's off Limits ... 24

Depriving Someone from Meeting Another ... 26

Second Chance ... 28

Destiny and Ruben Became Roommates ... 29

Does a Man Deserve a Chance? ... 31

Fatima and Mario ... 32

Friends Wanting the Same Man ... 34

Getting Together ... 35

Going the Distance ... 37

Happiness with Someone ... 40

Having Friends of the Opposite Sex ... 41

Having Something in Common ... 42

He Isn't Coming This Way ... 43

He's Sweet, Generous, and Hard-Working ... 44

Holly Refrains from Intimacy ... 45

How to Balance Having a Social Life ... 46

Is Money More Important to You?	47
It's All About Respect	49
It's Alright to Talk about Intimacy	50
Jillian Wanted What Was Best for Herself	51
Josephina Found Out the Truth	54
Just Looking	57
Ladies Night Out	58
Leaving Relationships Behind	60
Love is Questionable	61
Love or Lust?	64
Lynette's Secrecy	65
Marguerite Only Communicated Sometimes	67
Marriage Counseling	69
Marriage Ending in Divorce	70
Mary Gave Raymond a Chance	71
Megan's First Love	74
Mothers-In-Law	77
Nathaniel's Addiction to Lora	78
No Matter the Circumstances	80
Oh, She's the Mistress	81
Out of Sight Out of Mind	82
Pretender	84
Rekindle Your Intimate Desires	85
Remembering the First Time Together	86
Respecting Each Other's Time	87
Sasha is the Difficult Type	88
Secret Intimacy	89
She is an Urban Soldier	91
Shelly's Abrupt Ending from Troy	92
Silent Resentment and Anger	95
Sitting and Looking Beautiful	96
Starting Over	98
Sybil Didn't Want to Hear it	99

The Emotional Replay 101
The Flirtation Isn't Going Anywhere 102
They're Over Ninety and Still Together 104
There They Go Again 105
They Call Them Cougars 106
Trent Craved Marital Advice 107
Wanting Intimacy 109
Wanting the Whole Package 110
What is Your Dating Introduction? 111
When Your Intimacy isn't Private Anymore 112
Why Complain, Isn't Your Husband Working? 113
Wife, Mother, or Girlfriend 114
Yearning for Your Husband's Presence 115
You Can't Force Someone to Love You 116
You Must Have Dating Rules 117
Your Mate Isn't Affectionate Anymore 119

Introduction

People get into relationships that is always intriguing and complicated, without knowing the outcome. After meeting someone who could possible be a new husband, wife, girlfriend or significant other. There lives will change, especially if decidng to finally get married. Ultimately, many people do look forward to being happy, and to find someone to spend time with, isn't an easy goal for men and women looking for the right companion. Now a days, as they say, till death due us part isn't taken seriously. Even though, couples will get married, engaged or in a long-term or short-term relationship with someone new, can become questionable. For instance, there isn't a huge emphasis placed on the importance of being in a good relationship, but men and women continue seeking no matter what. Although, it's common that people are in and out of relationships that can be wonderful, unhealthy or misunderstood. No one wants to enter a relationship like a revolving door, but the experience will help in choosing a person who seems to be the one to feel comfortable with. Overall, couples love memorable times that can be cherished, but the constant change to enter in or out of relationships can be disappointing for people who just want happiness. The many unexpected issues can become tiresome for men and women who wish to be loved, and they'll wait for someone no matter how long it takes. The chances taken will become a journey, and not knowing when and where will be the time to meet someone new. Although life is filled with twist and turns. Everyone will know falling in and out of love will lead to being happy with someone over time.

A Man May Choose to Stay or Leave

Many women realize that their lives are very busy and having a relationship can be difficult because a man has many needs and desires from his woman when he is around her. A man may feel that he isn't getting the attention he deserves because women want to have it all: a family and a career. Some women aren't always aware of her man's every need. For example, many men and women have children from previous relationships, and a man can be content with his woman for a while, but slowly there can be problems if a man stays with a woman who doesn't have his biological children. Some men try to make it work, but it can become complicated to love a woman and her children, because it takes time to get to know everyone. Many women decide to wait to be with a man because he's not the father of her children, and there are some men who don't mind at all. Many women will continue their search for a man who shows signs of being comfortable about the situation. In addition, it can also be a pattern for a man to leave a woman, because she will not accept the man's children from a previous relationship.

Ultimately, most women will acknowledge that they'd prefer to be alone for a while until the children are adults. Many women would express to each other that they continue to experience, not having much luck with men due to family concerns. Most do prefer to have a long-term loving relationship, with a man who will eventually love the whole family.

A Ray of Sunshine

It was a bright Monday morning and Crystal was waiting for the bus to go to work. She wanted to share a story with her friend Lisa before getting to work, but she usually has conversations with Lisa on the weekends around her dinner table. She wanted to talk with Lisa about her neighbor, Alisha. Crystal spoke to her on Sunday before starting the work week, it was always a part of Crystal and Lisa's daily ritual to talk about acquaintances. They enjoy gossiping about people they know. One day, Crystal and Lisa were having their phone conversation. Crystal expressed concerns to Lisa about her neighbor, Alisha, speaking about a man who was doing some work on the roof next door.

Crystal began, "The man was watching Alisha from next door glancing at her face with a look of fascination. She was only getting some air and enjoying the sun's glare, but the man had a good reason. He was watching like her beauty was a ray of sunshine. He looked as if he was hypnotized just by looking at her. She said he was an unfamiliar new face in the neighborhood, only working on her neighbor's house. Alisha assumed he hadn't seen her around before, because of the way he was watching her. She said if he wasn't working on the roof next door, doing some repairs with other workers, he would have never seen her because a gate was blocking the next door neighbors' private view. Even though the man was working on the roof, he was trying to watch Alisha from a distance. She saw him watching, so she smiled at him and then turned her back, because she said it was amusing to see a man at eight in the morning looking at her with such an attraction and not saying a word. He was focused on her as if he was viewing a celebrity - with fascination. Although working on the roof should've been his only focus, he continued to stare until she walked away. Alisha said that she decided to go indoors to peek through her window and watch him work. Then, she saw him looking anxiously next door after she left, as if he was trying to see her face once again; he was watching her continuously, similar to viewing enjoyable entertainment that would come to an end. Eventually, she returned to the window periodically to look outside to see if he was still there by the end of the day. She tried to stay busy indoors, but will return to her window and saw that the roof next door was completely repaired. Then, she became curious if he could have been someone who was worth approaching, though he was gone after the sun went down."

"Alisha regretted not speaking to the man first although she felt that a man should always make the first move. It was the man's loss, because he only watched. He was obviously concerned about his co-workers being there, and he probably didn't know what to say. Overall, communication is essential."

Accepting Whatever Goes

Why do so many men and women who are involved in relationships accept dealing with "whatever goes" when being with someone of interest? Many couples cannot answer the question with a sure answer except for saying they are in love. No matter what a person does that is unacceptable in a relationship, staying and continuously accepting "whatever goes" can be contributed to many reasons. An individual will accept, to go through unhappy situations in a relationship due to low self-esteem and insecurities, and then will deal with issues such as verbal or physical abuse, cheating, and lack of communication. Furthermore, men and women have to be aware of what is going to be accepted and what isn't. It's important to have respect for yourself if you're familiar with the unacceptable behavior someone has shown from the beginning, because ignoring conflict can escalate. The mistreatment can be your fault if staying with an individual is too much to bear. Therefore, happiness with someone should only be shown on the faces of couples who are willing to try to be content. Everyone knows that no one is perfect and there isn't anything wrong with giving someone another chance before giving up. It's only a choice an individual can make, even though men and women want to be with someone who seems perfect. Relationships don't always work out that way, but meeting someone new is challenging and exciting from the beginning, but some men and women can become blind to difficulties. Only communication over "whatever goes" is the number one priority when being with someone.

Always Expecting Material Things

Giving and receiving a gift can be a beautiful thing to have something valuable, that was given from the person who is in love. Sometimes, a person may have urges for many material things. For example, some people will accept extravagant gifts such as a car, jewelry, furniture, appliances, or expensive trips. Gift-giving can be a test to find out if a person truly loves material things, or if there's actually love and appreciation, because some people stay in relationships just to have material things. Sometimes, people will recognize the behavior of someone who is only after what others can give. In some situations, the person who wants too much will leave the other if not receiving enough, and the relationship will eventually end. On the other hand, two people who have a strong bond will give each other things without acting as if giving is a priority and looking for more is secondary. Everyone loves beautiful things or traveling to beautiful places, but if there isn't love, then the relationship isn't going to work at all because no one enjoys being used. A person in love can be happy with or without material things, even though most men and women expect nice things on their birthday or holidays. As the saying goes, "it's the thought that counts," and complaining about wanting something better shouldn't be the focus. Having special gifts from someone and getting nice things, is a token of someone's love and interest. It shouldn't be a game to try to get something from someone who is just generous and kind.

Always Nonchalant

I have to admit that I've noticed that men are usually more nonchalant than women. It's the behavior that most men demonstrate, and women don't know what they are up to all the time. They are usually calm and quiet about matters that women show more concern for, such as where to go for a weekend trip or what should be worn at the up and coming party that a friend has planned. Even though men do have a nonchalant reaction to many things, it's actually a good characteristic. Many women will sometimes overreact and jump to conclusions when their husband or boyfriend didn't come home late, after visiting some friends or coming home late after a Christmas party that was held at work. There can be misunderstandings when a man is just going out to have a good time. Therefore, some men don't know what to expect from their women, after a night of fun. A man's nonchalant behavior can make a woman become suspicious sometimes. Whether it's a problem with her own insecurities that is getting the best of her or the pleasure of wanting to know what her man is doing constantly. Many women don't have enough trust in their men and some men may threaten to leave if she always doubts them. She will contemplate what he is saying and try to make it work if he has decided to leave, because a man who isn't doing anything wrong does not want to be accused. Furthermore, women and men who make their mate feel guilty about something untrue can leave the other person curious, and the stress of the accusation may push him to do something with someone else. Involving oneself with another person could result in regret, because of being nonchalant. Many couples sometimes find that there can be a problem if not expressing an exciting, enthusiastic response to anything. In time, men or women who show this behavior towards each other usually know that they shouldn't be complaining about everything. Having trust and communication is the best way to work towards having a stress free mind in a relationship.

What Impresses You?

When men and women meet, sometimes there's a chance that they'll try to impress the person they're interested in. Every now and then, they will go overboard to impress each other. Doing so can sometimes make an individual look like a fool, such as speaking loudly to be noticed or wearing unusual clothing that can grab the attention of the person looking. Impressing someone can be fun and exciting for some people, but for many men and women, being themselves is preferred. Many people would rather be with someone who knows about himself or herself. Instead of being with a person who is trying to act like someone they're really not. Do something that works and try being true to yourself first, before acting foolish. What may impress one person may not impress another.

Are You Ready for the Chase?

Do you have a time frame for waiting for intimacy? Well, many men and women would admit to holding off on being intimate. Some men and women would rather enjoy the chase before having the pleasure of an intimate encounter with someone new. Others will converse for months with someone face to face or over the phone, because of being interested to know the person as much as possible before anything more takes place. The chase makes everything more exciting, and the anticipation will slowly approach. In addition, doing fun things together such as enjoying long walks in the park and holding hands, or having fun creative romantic ideas to impress each other can be great when taking it slow. Meeting someone for the first time is exciting, but knowing when to leave each other after a date before things heat up is important. Give each other a pleasant hug, because being together too soon after becoming intimate wouldn't be ideal and the situation would become awkward. Then, you will have to acknowledge that the chase is officially over. Many people wonder why there isn't a returned phone call after being intimate too soon. Try and refrain from temptation if wanting a serious relationship with someone of interest.

Breaking Up Isn't Easy

What does an individual say to a boyfriend or girlfriend when it's time to break up. There isn't a perfect way to get the message across. Is it better to say it face to face, by phone, by text messaging, or by email? No matter how a person breaks up with someone, no one can foresee the outcome. Nobody wants to hear those words and many people don't know how to react when someone says, "I don't want you anymore, don't call ever again, you go your way and I'll go mine." Saying these words to someone can result in unpredictable behavior that is unusual for everyone involved. In some cases, a person can be in denial about the break up and can become vindictive or violent, towards the person conducting the break up, to become an extremely miserable person. The experience will be upsetting. There's feelings of confusion, anger, depression, suicidal behavior, and loneliness. Everyone handles a break up differently, so it's important to understand, if a person says, "it's over," then respect the other person's choice. It doesn't make sense to cause a complicated matter to escalate, because no one can make someone stay in a relationship, if there isn't happiness anymore. Therefore, making a person stay committed isn't the answer, be smart about your reaction after a break up, and allow yourself to let go of someone, if the relationship isn't the way it used to be. As they say, "time heals all wounds."

Business or Pleasure Trips

Neil is a twenty-eight year old, hard-working, educated man who landed the ultimate career in real-estate. He lives with his wife in Washington D.C., but this caused conflict with his wife, Loretta, because he would travel often. Unexpectedly, he'd have to pack his bags to get prepared for his flight again. It was exciting, but Neil's boss always ask him to go on business trips more often and Loretta assumed that the business ventures were all about business. But even though Neil loved his wife, he met someone on the job and had gotten to know a woman named Kenya. He had worked with her every day over the past three years, but Loretta didn't know anything about Neil's co-worker and love interest. He didn't expect anything would happen and he started getting home late at night. He made bogus plans sometimes and acted as if he was traveling alone, but Neil wanted to be with Kenya. Meanwhile, his wife Loretta was at home and had no idea what was going on. Loretta decided to make a phone call to Neil's job one day and Neil happened to pick up.

Loretta said, "I just wanted to tell you that I miss your voice and presence throughout the day." Surprisingly, when Neil responded to Loretta, he mistakenly called her Kenya.

Neil tried to cover his tracks by saying, "I mistakenly called you by my clients' name who is supposed to come this morning for a meeting in my office."

Loretta brushed it off and asked when he would be home. Neil said, "The same time as usual, I'll call you when I'm on my way okay babe, bye." Loretta had some suspicion and wasn't her usual self over the phone, because Neil abruptly said the wrong name. Even though, Loretta didn't make a huge deal out of the matter, but there had been more unusual behavior from Neil, such as leaving home in the evening, or going out more often on the weekends. The disappointment started to become a reality to Loretta, because she knew for sure that Neil was seeing someone else. So, Loretta decided to get her mind off of him by going to see a movie with her best friend, Melody, the following weekend.

On Saturday, Loretta and Melody were happy to spend some time out. As they both entered Melody's car on their way to the movie theater, Loretta started talking a lot about Neil and the possibility that he was seeing someone else. Melody wanted Loretta to get her mind off of Neil for a little while, Melody said, "Let's talk about Neil after we see the movie. I don't want you to be upset, let's just enjoy the movie we're going to see."

As they drove up to the parking lot of the movie theater, they got out of the car to stand on line. Suddenly, Loretta saw Neil walking towards her with a female friend to get in the ticket line. Loretta was looking, but she didn't expect what she saw. Loretta decided she wasn't going to walk away, because she wanted to face them both. She said, "Hi Neil, who is this?" He answered her and Loretta continued to say, "You have finally introduced me to the person who has taken the free time that should've been for both of us, right?" Loretta tried to keep her composer, but surprisingly, Kenya said that they had been seeing each other for some time now. Loretta was shocked and just stared at both of them, and didn't say a word. She was disappointed and the expression was shown on her face as she looked over at her friend. Then, she walked towards the car with Melody, because she was in shock about what had happened; she didn't even bother to see the movie. When driving away, she seemed to be confused and distracted and she started speeding as fast as she could. Melody asked Loretta to pull over, so she could drive instead. Loretta said okay and pulled over, but she was silent throughout the whole ride. When she finally arrived at home, she decided to pack Neil's bags. She also decided to leave a letter on the table about her disappointment in him cheating and lying. Loretta never wanted to see his face again, so Melody offered her to stay over until she was ready to return home. Loretta thought it was a great idea, because she needed some time away from Neil to think.

Finally, when Loretta decided to go home after he was gone, she saw that everything Neil had owned was also gone. Even though Loretta had mixed feelings about him, there was a sigh of relief that she made the right choice to let him go. Loretta realized she needed to start a new chapter in her life. So the following morning, Loretta called Melody once again to talk about what was going on at home, but before hanging up, Loretta said, "no woman should allow herself to settle for less if she isn't happy, and I will find someone new. Many people do make it through the storm no matter what the outcome is in many relationships. I'm not going to give up, because love is worth another try. Thanks for listening; I'm not going to take up all your time, so I'll call you tomorrow, bye."

❦ Charlotte's Unfair Financial Situation ❦

Charlotte is a responsible, thirty-eight year old woman who lives in Revere, Massachusetts. She is single, and she has three daughters. Shelby is twelve, Jocelyn is ten, and Lucy is five years old. They are the love of Charlotte's life, and she would do anything for them. She is a nurse who works very hard, but she is trying to also progress in an online boutique business. Although things were moving slowly, she thought of good ideas that could help her with her thriving business, so she continued to invest small amounts of money towards her goal. She was in a financial bind, because she wanted more for her daughters. She would communicate with her daughter's fathers, Maxwell and Emmitt, who lived in the same state. They would show up at her door separately to help when they could. Eventually, she was getting somewhere slowly with her Boutique business. There were times that she appeared to be doing well with her work, but the fathers would take back what she was entitled to for her daughters when Charlotte became more independent. She didn't seem to need to ask for help as much as she used to, but even though the fathers didn't know each other, it was unusual that they were withholding funds from her because of the same reason. They both assumed that Charlotte was selfish about how she was using the finances given. She didn't think she needed to tell them that she had something bigger in mind for her daughters. She wanted to have something waiting for her daughters as they became adults. She was proud to be working towards that accomplishment, but she was disappointed that both of the fathers ended their relationships in the past for the same purpose, due to the high cost of caring for their daughters. Occasionally, Charlotte would talk to her mother, Doris, about her financial issues. One day, unexpectedly, Charlotte's mom wanted to visit, to see what her daughter and grandchildren were up to. Charlotte seemed desperate to speak to her mom right away. They both sat down on the couch, and the girls gave their mom some time to talk to their grandmother.

"Mom, I really need to talk. I'm so tired of being the only one doing everything for my daughters. Maxwell and Emmitt are no longer giving me any funds for the girls. They both will constantly pressure and proposition me separately to be intimate and if I didn't respond to their request, then the girls wouldn't receive what they're entitled to. I'm moving ahead in my life and I'm not giving in to either one. It was difficult to tell you the entire truth, and why the fathers started losing interest in supporting the girls. What matters to me the most is to be the best mother I could be for my daughter's sake."

Doris said, "You're right Charlotte, but as long as you know what you want, everything you're doing for Shelby, Jocelyn, and Lucy will eventually work out fine. Even though it seems that Maxwell and Emmitt just want to be spiteful, it's a coincidence that both of them never met, but feel the same way."

"I was also surprised by their behavior but I never spoke to either one about the other. I only wanted to confide in you about it. Furthermore, I'm not a person who has a strong love for money, but not telling them how I felt about the issue, affected my finances for the girls. I feel that it's important to get along with the fathers no matter what. Although, without question, a father is supposed to be there for a mother when she is dealing with a lot of important issues alone and it's a good idea to have a plan "B" when everything starts to fall apart financially."

"You're right," Doris said, "As long as you know what you are doing for your daughters long-term, that's all that matters. Everything will work itself out, but I think that you shouldn't bring up the subject about money to them anymore, because I don't want you to worry yourself. Just understand that I'm there for you and we can just work together, to take care of the girls, and in time they'll come around when they're ready, because as the saying goes: "Money Isn't Everything."

Cheating Debate

Why do so many men and women complain about a mate who has cheated? Some people don't understand why a person will cheat. Many men and women feel that the behavior is forbidden and difficult to accept. Many people who are in relationships do not want to deal with cheating. A large percentage of individuals do engage in this behavior, that will cause someone to be in denial about what their mate is doing when no one is around. On the other hand, there are men and women who accept this behavior from their mate and are okay with the idea of dating many people. It isn't something that works out for everyone and being open can come with a price, but some people do believe it is a healthy way to keep a relationship together. Whatever men and women feel about cheating, we all have to accept that it isn't something that human beings can eliminate completely. It's a temptation that everyone have to contemplate on often, and some men and women have to live with their own choices when cheating. As long as people are acting upon feelings of desire, the cheating debate will continue throughout our lives.

Couple's Private Bedroom Conversations

Many couples feel comfortable enough with each other to talk about almost anything on their minds, especially in the privacy of their own bedroom. They may share the same issues with some family members or close friends, but many couples prefer to only have private bedroom conversations they can cherish dearly. They may not want to talk about personal issues with family and friends, because some people find that sharing everything with their family and friends can be problematic. Their relationship wouldn't be private anymore, and speaking about a problem can cause a strain in a couple's happy relationship. There can be a huge misunderstanding if people who necessarily shouldn't be involved get involved, and then what was expressed will become the couple's fault for choosing to share their bedroom conversations. Some women will say what they feel is important, and will not care who is around, when being upset about their mate. What was said can come back to them with some regret, because her man may not know what is being said about him, because he isn't present. Everyone needs someone to confide in about difficult subjects. These discussions should be worked out amongst couples, before sharing personal information with the people in their lives, because some couples can become confused about staying together, separating, or breaking up completely. In addition, a man can also find himself seeking advice from his family and friends. He may drift away from the love of his life, just to be in the arms of another woman who is willing to listen without judging his relationship. Over time, the other woman will become attached, because of what he is telling her. So it's important for long-term couples to keep their relationships private to some extent. Only two people in love know the full story.

Crystal Tried to Move on From Kirk

Crystal and Kirk met at a thirty-something neighborhood bar in Providence, Rhode Island. They dated for a while, but there wasn't any long-term commitment. They assumed what they had would last, but there wasn't any chemistry. After two weeks, Kirk decided to visit Crystal unexpectedly and she was uncomfortable about him showing up at her home. Kirk rang her doorbell just to see how she was doing. Crystal opened the door and saw that he was looking rather well groomed as if he wanted to get together. She knew what he wanted, but she didn't want to lead him on too strongly. It wasn't her personality to make the first move and tell him what she was thinking. She acted as if she wasn't interested, but she still has feelings for him. Furthermore, Crystal called her friend, Dona, to talk about Kirk after he left. She immediately said that it was difficult for her to get over Kirk. "I looked at him from head to toe when he came over, because he was looking rather scrumptious like a hot piece of pie waiting to be eaten."

Dona replied, "Composure is important. It's best because you know what you both had didn't work out."

"He wants me back, and that was the reason for his visit, but I need to have self-control. I want to accept turning him down, and I want to keep my word. After leaving him, I was single again, but I'm okay, and I didn't plan on looking back; I have unresolved feelings, but I'm going to do what is right. So I only looked and I didn't want to entice him in any way; turning him down is all I did, even though I ended my relationship." Crystal surprisingly said to Dona, "I've met a new man through a mutual friend of mine name Bridgette. I decided to go on a blind date and now we're together. I'm going to continue dating Irvin, because we enjoy each other's company. I hope it works out, and I don't plan on breaking up with him any time soon. I hope he doesn't treat me like a fool. Right now, it's going great; all I want is to be content with Irvin, and hopefully, my feelings for Kirk will diminish, because all I want is to be happy with Irvin without being in denial for wanting Kirk back."

Dona answered, "You already have a man who cares for you now. I believe in time you will get over Kirk. Time heals all wounds."

Daphne's Love for Eric

It was a hot summer night in Los Angeles, California, so Daphne and Joanne spoke about going out for a night on the town. They were close sisters, but they didn't see each other often. Daphne had some vacation time and she wanted a break from her career as a social worker in Massachusetts, so Joanne invited Daphne to stay with her for summer vacation. Joanne was a fashion designer in Los Angeles and she is a very busy person, and when they met at the airport, they were excited to see each other. As Daphne walked off the airplane, she saw Joanne and they both were so happy that they ran up to see each other and hugged, but all they talked about, was going to the nearest neighborhood bar/restaurant to sit and relax to have dinner and a drink. They wanted to catch up on what had been going on in their lives. They didn't speak to each other on the phone often, because they'd rather talk in person. They enjoyed their conversation, meanwhile, waiting for dinner, and they talked about many subjects. Daphne started out by saying, "I'm glad that we can talk. I've been dealing with a lot at work and it's a nice change of pace."

Joanne replied, "I really appreciate you coming to see me, even though I'm always so busy. I'm continuously looking for the next hot fashion design, but you know what? We're here to have a good time, so let's see if we can try to have a little fun through-out the night."

Eventually, they started to observe some of the men looking for company and conversation, but the sisters were more absorbed with bonding to catch up on what was going on in their lives. When they knew the night was coming to an end, they didn't have a ride home from the bar, so they decided to call a cab. There was a man from the same bar who overheard that Daphne and Joanne were having difficulty finding a cab outside. The man decided to approach them and ask if they needed a ride home. He told them his name was Eric and he was a regular at that bar. Then, Daphne and Joanne said to Eric, that they will like a ride home. As they all walked towards his Mercedes-Benz, Daphne whispered to Joanne that Eric was interested in one of them. While in the car, Eric didn't hesitate to ask Daphne for her phone number. He seemed to be attracted to her and she was also attracted to him. When Eric arrived at their destination, Daphne and Joanne got out of his car. Then, Eric said, he will call Daphne tomorrow, and he will see them both again sometime soon.

Daphne was anticipating Eric's phone call, but Eric didn't call Daphne for about a week. When he finally did call, she was excited to hear his deep voice over the phone. He called to make arrangements to get together for the following weekend. When they eventually started dating, they did everything together every weekend for months. She would call her sister on the phone to talk about Eric all the time. She also express her deepest feelings to her closest friends. Kim, Julie, and Gabrielle, who reside in Los Angles. During the week, Daphne decided to see her friends at the same bar/restaurant to have a drink and talk.

Daphne started out by saying, "Eric seems to be like the perfect dream come true, and I will like my closest friends to be happy for me." They looked at each other strangely when Daphne described him. Daphne asked them, why did they look at each other suspiciously? They didn't say a word. After weeks passed, then everything started to change between Daphne and Eric, and when the weekends approached, they will see each other less and less. Eric, for some reason, seemed to avoid Daphne's phone calls, and then she will call her sister Joanne to talk, and after her sister answered.

Daphne said, "It's possible that Eric is starting to lose interest in going out on the weekends with me. I've gotten used to his lifestyle, and I became a part of his circle of friends. It was exciting for a while, but I didn't understand why Eric was becoming distant from me. Eric didn't give me an explanation, about why he was losing interest, because I thought everything was going well. He started to make me feel unappreciated and used. I do not want to accept it and move on."

Joanne responded, "It sounds like you're starting to become obsessed with Eric, aren't you?"

"Maybe, because he left me confused, I just want some answers. I find myself looking for him all the time at the bar he frequents. I don't want to accept that he is trying to avoid me; I also call him all the time. I even started to ask around town if anyone had seen him, but no one will give me any information."

Joanne said, logically, "Try to get over him because if he isn't interested anymore, don't force him to be with you. If you want, we can go out together until you find another man."

"I'm not interested in finding a new man right away; I think I just need some time to figure out what I'm going through, before I can date again." Eventually, Daphne started to sink into a deep depression about how Eric had treated her. She also lost a lot of weight because she thought about him all the time. She continued speaking to her sister and friends about the intimacy and passion she once had for Eric, but Daphne decided she will go out once again on a Saturday night to find the man she thought was hers.

When arriving at the bar, she was anxious with excitement because she finally saw him. But she was suddenly surprised to see him with another woman. Daphne was heartbroken and she knew what she had with Eric was over, but she kept herself together without causing a scene, because it was important for her not to allow herself to lose control. She decided to leave the bar alone after seeing Eric's raunchy behavior, and dirty dancing with another woman in front of her face. Finally, Daphne decided to speak to her friends about what had happened. They surprisingly admitted to her that they heard rumors that Eric was a lady's man. They told Daphne that they didn't want to hurt her feelings. They all suggested she should find out for herself. Daphne wasn't angry with her friends for not telling her, but the situation became understandable to her, about being rejected so abruptly. After Daphne saw what was going on with Eric, and after her heart was broken. Speaking to her sister Joanne every day was helpful for her after returning to Massachusetts. Daphne took months to get over him, so she will call Joanne to talk about him, because her feelings were diminishing slowly. Now, Daphne is more aware about the next man she gets involved with, although she will always remember Eric.

Darrel's Forbidden Entry and Exit

Noreen is a thirty-five year old woman who works as a receptionist at a hair salon in her neighborhood community. One day, as she was on her way home from work in Peabody, Massachusetts, she received a phone call from her friend Darrel. He wanted to know how she was doing, but his intention was for something more. Darrel wanted to spend some private time with Noreen because she hadn't been intimate with him for about three months. Darrel continued to talk about being intimate with her once again when she had time. Although she knew he was involved with someone else. Occasionally, she will see him if she decided to, because Noreen and Darrel were also friends. She will tell her best friend Courtney about Darrel, when they will see each other Saturday evenings for dinner.

Noreen said, "I planned on cutting all ties with Darrel because what I'm doing just doesn't feel right to me at all. Especially, when he will enter and exit my place as if he was guilty and suspicious. I will continue to see him when I wanted to and he wouldn't give up on me, because he also enjoyed spending time with me. But everytime he will see me, he seemed guilty for visiting "secretly," and after arriving at my doorstep, I will look out the door suspiciously after he entered, and he'll do the same. Darrel looked around as if he thought someone was following him to my house. After, he'd become more relaxed at my house, we'll talk for a while, but Darrel acted as if he had more important things on his mind, so he will leave me rapidly. After our intimate encounters, he will give me a kiss, and then say goodbye. I always felt uncomfortable when he exited my house, as if he were leaving a forbidden place. I understood that Darrel will have to go back to his significant other, after he leaves and we wouldn't see each other for a while; being involved with him will always be the same because I know that it's all about wanting one thing."

Courtney responded, "You're in a situation that doesn't seem honest and healthy. You're only pretending about what you have with him is going somewhere. You know that Darrel is already with someone. I hope that you move on because Noreen, you're my friend and I think you can spend time with someone who isn't worried about entering your house and being followed."

"I'm not happy about what I've gotten myself into, but I know what I'm doing. I accepted what we were doing, because I didn't want to know all the specifics about his life. Whenever Darrel felt that he wanted to share anything with me, he would and vice versa. But in the midst of our last conversation, I did tell him that I planned on leaving to make a career change, and I'll be moving away to California to pursue singing. Darrel didn't respond after I told him, but I'm positive that there isn't anymore deception; I do want to end his guilt. I have control over the situation to end it completely."

"Back up, wait a minute, you didn't tell me that you were moving to California."

"I know I didn't tell you right away but yes, I'm definitely going. I just have to work on some things before I go, you're welcome to come along if you like."

"I have to think about it, but you need to work things out for yourself; especially the situation with Darrel. I think moving away from him will make your life a lot less difficult, but I'm going to miss you. I will visit you in California when you're settled; just don't continue the pattern you left behind in the first place. Understand that you're worth more than that; stay focused on your career. Eventually you'll meet someone better."

Noreen finished with, "I love you Courtney for being there no matter what life has in store." Then, Noreen got out of her seat to give Courtney a hug and they both prepared to go home after having a delicious dinner.

Denise Said He's off Limits

Denise is the type of woman who doesn't want to lose her man. She's always looking out the corner of her eye, assuming her boyfriend, Dillon, is always interested in other women. She can be insecure about herself and doesn't want her man to leave her for another woman. She is known to tell other women, "Don't even look at my man, he's off limits." She is controlling and thinks she has all the answers about what a woman wants from her man. She will do and say anything just to keep him with her, but he likes the attention she gives him when she is upset. Denise expresses herself to her family and friends, but speaks in a selfish controlling way, acting as if she knows her man isn't always dishonest. She always asks him where he's been, because she just wants to enjoy spending time with him. Often, her time is spent keeping females away and she'll tell them that her man is off limits. No matter what she says or does, Dillon will still do what he wants when she isn't around, her agenda is to control her man's every move whenever she thinks she can. She say anything disrespectful to women to get them to stay away from him, because she wants to keep her man from leaving her. Even though Dillon is seen by many people who say that he enjoys getting around, he doesn't care about what anyone thinks. He is a narcissistic person who only cares about what he wants and nothing will stop him, not even her. Denise has spent many years approaching any woman, she knew for sure her man had been with, because she will invade his personal information on his cell phone and will call his other women just to tell them all, what she thought. Her explosive outbursts would appear to be outlandish to express all her thoughts. She would "argue" about what the women he was involved with put her through. She'll forget that he started the mess, because he would keep secrets from her; he knew she will be hurt if she found out. Many women he'll be involved with didn't even know, the Denise type actually exist. She will "argue" with one of his women on his cell phone. After everything was said, the advice from the other woman will be: "If a man is making you unhappy, then you shouldn't have to be with him. Find a way to be happy with yourself and if he loves you, he wouldn't put you through this, so find someone who doesn't like playing games, because you're only making yourself look foolish. Do yourself a favor, clear your head and start all over again for your own sake and talk to someone who can help." Suddenly, the disrespect changed to respect, about what the other woman had to say. The Denise type will admit that her man did put her through a lot, and she will consider what was said by the other woman; she'd apologize for her behavior and then they'd just hang up, because there's nothing more to say.

Depriving Someone from Meeting Another

What is wrong with being honest from the beginning before you lead someone on to believe that there isn't someone else in your life? Many men and women are committed to someone, but sometimes become selfish and tell the next person of interest what they want to hear. Depriving someone from getting serious with another person who is single, can become dishonest to the person who isn't seeing anyone. Men and women do hope to be with someone who isn't married, or committed to a significant other. Seeing someone else is common among many men and women who are already taken. For example, when a man walks up to a woman and says, "Hi, how are you doing? What is your name?" A woman will be polite enough to say what her name is, but she would hope that the man she have interest for isn't going to confess that there is someone else. When men and women fabricate sometimes after introducing themselves. They'll have the audacity to look the person of interest directly in the eye and say there isn't anyone special in my life at the moment. In some cases, there are many men and women who are honest and would usually admit that they have someone before putting themselves in another situation, because they don't want to have any regrets. Sometimes when someone involved finds out about being lied to, then the relationship will end abruptly, because most people do not accept deception. Although the person who deceived you is someone you're still attracted to, and you will continue to see the other person for a while. Furthermore, many people will consider moving on, because of untruthfulness from the beginning. It just becomes an unfair situation for someone who is involved, after meeting someone for the first time. Trying to accept starting over again if finding out that the person you're seeing is committed to someone else can be difficult. Some men and women will fail to admit what he or she has done wrong from the beginning, but many happy couples will share relationship concerns with family or friends who are unhappy continuously about never being in love. Eventually, men and women going through this will try to learn how to trust again, and wouldn't accept giving up on love completely. It's extremely helpful to always ask concerning questions from the beginning before possibly dealing with regret that will follow if not wanting to deal with unacceptable behavior, because no one wants to be unhappy and confused without a reason. Men and women who are in denial will endure the dishonesty that isn't making anything better.

Second Chance

Do you know it is time to be with someone new, but don't know what to expect? Do you want love, attention, and affection, but not the pain that follows? It's exciting to meet a new person who loves getting together to have fun, laugh, and everything that comes in between, but suddenly, everything ends unexpectedly. The rejection will hurt to the point of no return to happiness felt before meeting this person. You try to gather what was said throughout the relationship, such as what was expressed at the beginning when dating and the signs that should result to end dating someone new. Then the guessing game will make it hard to comprehend what has happened, because trying to connect the dots becomes impossible for many men and women. He or she will ask, "What happened? Don't treat me this way. Give me a chance; don't I deserve that last chance?" The frustration of not being loved in return can cause a person to move slowly again before starting over, because of unanswered questions that many will experience, and will ask once again. "What happened to us? Don't treat me this way; don't I deserve a second chance? What is it? Are you looking for perfection and or material things?" Leading for one to also say, "I don't have it all, but love is what I have to offer you. Don't you want to be with someone who can be there for you? I know making it work takes time, be patient and you'll see that I'm the one who can make you happy for eternity."

Destiny and Ruben Became Roommates

Destiny and Ruben were reminiscing about old times with their friends Diana and Lionel over dinner. They spoke about the memories they had as far back as they could remember. Destiny had asked everyone to come over and sit by the fireplace. She wanted to talk about how she and Ruben became best friends.

"We met each other in a church in Hartford, Connecticut. We both enjoyed singing in church on Sundays, and eventually we started to go to middle school and high school together. We seemed to always meet at school in the hallways and would be so excited to see each other. We became best friends and as the years passed and we became closer, we thought it will be a good idea to live together. We didn't have any interest in being intimate; we only wanted to be good friends. When we did decide to move in together, everything seemed great for us both at first, but eventually things slowly started to change between us. Having responsibilities started to change a once happy friendship, into roommates arguing about many things that we never thought will be a problem. Then I became set in my own ways, I had to be in control, have everything in order, and make sure bills were paid on time. On the other hand, Ruben started to slack off and soon after, he lost his job. I became unaccepting and refused to stay at the apartment where responsibilities weren't being met, so I decided that I would move out, but I left Ruben to pay all of the remaining balance on the bills. In the meantime, we both continuously complained. Eventually, we went our separate ways after coming to an agreement to pay the bills in the apartment, but we didn't want to end our friendship completely due to the problems of living together; the best decision was to remain friends. Even though we were childhood friends, we knew that being friends of the opposite sex wasn't an easy relationship to maintain."

Ruben chimed in, "We decided that remaining best friends was important to us, and we didn't want to become roommates ever again. Destiny and I didn't like to have tension, and our unconditional bond will last forever. It's great to be best friends, but everything can change when rushing into living together. Friendships shouldn't end if taking on responsibilities together. The result in doing so will cause an abrupt ending, which can become disappointing. So starting over by communicating and working things out without having any hard feelings towards each other is worth it."

Finally, Diana and Lionel glanced at each other, and then they looked back at Destiny and Ruben. Lionel said, "We appreciate your story; it's great, because to have best friends of the opposite sex is definitely not at all easy."

Does a Man Deserve a Chance?

There are women who are with men they're in love with, but do not trust and speak negatively about him to family and friends, because he may have been dishonest; she can be in denial that the relationship is just fine. Many women do put themselves in a situation with a dishonest man who doesn't share personal information, he's experienced before and after being in the relationship, but women like to know as much as possible. Some women will admit when being with someone long-term, there is a possibility of finding out something upsetting about the man they're committed to, for example, he has been intimate with someone of the same sex or has been with someone who has done time in prison for many years. In addition, a man will have done the ultimate unacceptable cheating behavior, and finding out about a child who has been born out of wedlock by another woman in the past or present. It's disappointing for many women to find out that their husband or boyfriend is the father of a secret child. Rebuilding the relationship will be difficult, but some couples remain together because they love each other dearly, but many men and women have skeletons in their closet and do not wish to tell their significant other every detail of their life. When the truth comes out, it can be shocking if something like this happens. The turmoil can be hard, when a woman is in love with her man. They'll consider giving their men another chance, because if not giving someone another chance can actually hurt just as much. Otherwise, if the relationship is worth another try, work it out in a mature manner; it's a lot easier than to continuously be hurt and angry. A woman should attempt to give the relationship a second try if she isn't ready to move on. Especially if she isn't going to leave her man anyway.

Fatima and Mario

Fatima and Olivia both lived in Winthrop, Massachusetts, and they spoke to each other every weekend. Fatima decided she will invite her friend Olivia over for Sunday brunch to talk about how they would spend their Saturday night. When Olivia arrived at Fatima's home, she rang the doorbell. Fatima opened the door with excitement and said, "Hi. I'm glad you came over; sit down, I'll get your meal for you."

Olivia returned with, "I'm happy that we can get to talk some more in person about our weekend."

"I was planning on staying in next weekend. I wasn't going to do much; only spending time at home cleaning and reading. Anyway, I wanted to tell you about a man I met a month ago at a neighborhood club that I go to alone sometimes after work, but I wanted talk to you face to face about him. He is a handsome man who has hazel brown eyes, beautiful light brown complexion, and he was attracted to me. When I started to speak to him, I was unable to get to know him and I felt that we had a big problem. The language barrier made it difficult to get to know him, because the man spoke very little English. He introduced himself as Mario and said he is from Panama, but he couldn't express himself fully to continue communicating in English. I became disappointed because I knew for sure that it wasn't going to work long-term if I did give Mario a chance, but I have to confide in you about something. I just started dating Mario, I became intimate with him, and I did enjoy being with him. I know that I'm a mature adult, but I have to admit that being with Mario intimately kept me interested for a while. He moves so quickly, I also met his family and his friends after we were together. I think he really likes me, but only a few of his family members spoke English. A few times I've met them, I felt out of place."

Suddenly, there was an unexpected knock at Fatima's door. She excused herself from the table to open the door and Fatima saw Mario looking at her lustfully. Mario said, "Hi. I surprised you, can I come in?"

Fatima said yes and introduced him to Olivia. After introductions, Mario followed with, "But I leave now, my friend in car waiting for me." Fatima understood and thanked him for stopping by, promising to call him later. After he left, Fatima asked Olivia what she thought of him.

"I see the connection between you both, and I see the way he looks at you. I hope you and Mario stay together; he seems like a nice man."

Olivia decided to go home and they both got up from around the table, hugged, and then went their separate ways.

Surprisingly, Fatima confessed to Olivia that she was ending her six year relationship with Mario. "We ended our relationship due to the challenge of the language barrier, because it's always frustrating trying to continuously understand each other. I thought the relationship will work out, but I wanted to be realistic about the situation. I felt like I needed to just let go, because I think it's best for Mario to fall in love with someone who will cater to his every needs. Especially, a woman who will also be his best friend and communicate with him in his own language. Hopefully, he will learn English as a second language, just to make things easier for himself. I will always have feelings for Mario despite the language barrier."

Olivia replied with, "I know it must be hard for you to end your relationship with Mario this way, but I'm here if you would like to talk."

"Don't become too concerned about me, I'll be alright. I'll talk to you later."

Friends Wanting the Same Man

It's common for two friends to have their eye on the same man at a party or a special event. Sometimes a man will approach both women, if he sees them watching him, but wherever a man meets a woman, sometimes an unusual, awkward predicament that is unexpected, for girlfriends who are both interested. When being in this type of situation, it can be a learning experience to know what a close friend is really like when a new guy comes along. Both friends may fuss about who will get him first, because of the same strong attraction towards him. The situation can become a competition between friends who have no idea from the beginning that conflict will occur. He may not be obvious who he's interested in more, so the situation can become complicated if a man doesn't say anything. Friends going through this should be aware of the signs; figure out who he's connected with from the beginning. The more interest a man shows one friend over the other is a clear sign; both friends should pay close attention to his flirtation towards one friend over the other. It's also important to ask the man from the beginning, which friend he is more interested in. Hopefully, both friends have a strong bond to accept his decision, because losing a good friend over a man shouldn't happen. Many friendships will become stronger through something like this. If a man comes in between a friendship, then only mature friends will get past it and continue to still be friends no matter what happens.

Getting Together

Tammy is a thirty-five year old who lives in Beverly, Massachusetts and she owns a high heel shoe store, but, she needed some time to socialize, so she decided to meet with her closest friends to talk about her weekend. Including, a man name Robert who she knows for nine years. Her friends, Amy and Macy, didn't know him, because Tammy was always private about her male relationships. She made plans to meet with them for dinner at her favorite restaurant on a Saturday night, to tell them about difficulties she was accepting from Robert. She wanted to finally talk about it because she started to realize that something didn't feel right to her anymore. She was always busy and she only preferred to speak about her serious personal matters when she could meet with her friends face to face. When they finally showed up at the restaurant looking beautiful, they had a seat around the dinner table. First of all, Amy and Macy engaged in small talk about what was going on in their own lives, but Tammy didn't express her feelings until after they all enjoyed eating dinner. After everyone was finished eating, the waiter approached the dinner table and took all their plates away. Then, he brought back a bottle of wine and glasses; Tammy decided she was going to open the bottle and pour the wine. As they all decided to sip on a glass of wine, Tammy proceeded to get her friends' attention. Without any hesitation Tammy said, "The man I've been seeing for nine years is married."

Amy expressed her feelings first. "What? You mean to tell me that the man you say is the love of your life is married?"

"Yes, I'm ending what we had. I only wanted to be honest and admit that I enjoyed being with him, but he is in a committed loving relationship to his wife Belinda. Robert is a passionate, understanding, and extremely affectionate man, but I want my relationship with him to end. My goal isn't to hurt Belinda's feelings. Robert has been in love with me and Belinda for years, I'm slowly falling out of love with him because I know this is wrong. I have called Robert to tell him to try and just get over me. Robert said he doesn't want to accept that it's over between us, and he said if that's how I want it to be, he'll respect that. I knew deep down inside what we have been living a lie for years involving, deception, secrecy, and infidelity. His wife Belinda didn't even know what was going on, and I'm sure if she did, she would not want to be a part of this. Anyway, Robert was silent on the phone and he hung up on me after we spoke. He didn't sound as if he had any guilt about the situation. So, what should I do?"

Amy replied, "I think that you should get out of the relationship before things get worse, because you're leading him on - you're letting him have his cake and eat it too."

"You're right, which is why I needed to meet with my friends to talk about what was going on in my relationship. I know I can eventually meet someone who will love me without getting involved in a predicament such as this. I want to have a higher expectation for myself, because that's the only way to move on. Even though I cared a lot for Robert, I did lead him on to believe that he can do what he wanted with me. I also knew it wasn't fair to Robert's wife Belinda, although she did not know me."

Finally, Macy intervened. "Both you and Robert have been living with the secrecy of infidelity. It's important not to let it happen again. Robert should get some counseling on how to become a better husband to his wife, because he will be living with the guilt for a very long time, unless he decides to express his feelings honestly to Belinda. It's his responsibility to communicate about what he's been doing. Telling the truth will be his choice, when he feels the time is right, because as they say 'the truth will set you free.'"

Then, Tammy said, "I have to admit that I do have great friends in my life. Thank you Amy and Macy."

Going the Distance

Ronda is a thirty-six year old woman who is new to Chicago from Philadelphia; she wanted to explore by moving to a new environment. After she arrived, she needed to know more about the area, so she decided to go out to become more familiar with Chicago, and she happen to meet a woman name Francesca. They met at a corner bus stop and started having a conversation. Francesca started with, "Excuse me, where did you purchase those beautiful high heeled boots? I like them."

"I'm from Philadelphia, and that's where I purchased them."

After introducing themselves, Francesca decided to ask Ronda, if she wanted to exchange cell phone numbers. Ronda agreed, and Francesca continued to say, "Call me when you want to learn your way around."

After meeting, they became good friends and did everything together. Eventually, when out doing some shopping, Francesca asked Ronda if she had a man.

Rhonda replied, "No, I wanted to get my life together first before thinking about a man."

Francesca said, "You know, I can be a good friend by looking for a nice gentleman for you to meet."

Ronda answered, "I'm not interested in anyone right now. I can wait, but if I'm in the presence of a man who seems interesting, then I will go out on a date if he asks."

However, it was a hot summer day and Francesca and Ronda needed to go to the nearest supermarket, to prepare for their weekend dinner. They wanted to celebrate their new friendship. Meanwhile, as they approached the supermarket. They had an additional conversation about dating, because Francesca was concerned that her friend Ronda was always alone without a man in her life. Ronda was not particularly interested in anyone and she felt that she was fairly new in

Chicago, so she wanted to take it slow. But, numerous times, Francesca will become persistent to look for someone for her. Ronda continued to say to Francesca, "I've given up on relationships temporarily. I don't know why you feel like you have to continuously pry into my personal life. I told you, if there is a man who meets my interests, I'll go out with him. I just like to take it slow, that's all."

Meanwhile, as they proceeded to go through the checkout line, there was an attractive man with a nice noticeable smile watching Ronda briefly browse through a magazine. Francesca was at the checkout line in front of Rhonda, so she saw the man looking at her. Francesca had a look in her eyes as if she knew he would be considered a candidate for Ronda to date. After Ronda was done scanning the magazine, she looked up and noticed the man watching her. She gave the man a smile, but she only wanted to leave the store after her checkout, and before they both exited the market, Francesca spontaneously decided to write down Ronda's phone number to give to the man without Ronda's permission.

Francesca went up to him and said, "Hi, I just wanted to give you my friend's phone number."

The man said, "Alright, I'll take it if she doesn't mind."

Francesca assured him that she doesn't. Ronda saw and overheard what Francesca had done and she acted as if she was a bit embarrassed. Ronda said to Francesca, "I can't believe what you've just done, you're lucky I don't mind that he has my number, because he is cute."

The man proceeded to checkout his items. He looked at the number and said to Ronda, "I'll call you alright."

Rhoda said okay, but immediately turned her head and said to Francesca, "He seems to have the intention of actually asking me for my cell phone number himself, but, Francesca, you beat him to it."

"I just hope that you both keep in touch, because he seems like a gentleman," Francesca replied.

The man decided to call Ronda and he told her that his name was Ralph. He was nervous the first time he saw Ronda, so he forgot to introduce himself properly. Eventually, they started to get to know each other better, because of spending a lot of time out together, but unexpectedly their happy relationship comes to an end after a year. Overall, Ronda wanted to return to her home town of Philadelphia; she missed everyone she knew. Most of her family and friends resided there, so she anticipated returning home. When Ronda traveled back to Philadelphia, she called Francesca.

"I needed to talk to you. When Ralph and I were saying goodbye at the airport, and as I was leaving to walk away, he said he will continue to communicate with me. Ralph always had deep feelings for me, so he plans on visiting when he has vacation time from his job as a construction worker, but I'm starting to feel that it isn't the same after leaving you and Ralph, after I returned home I felt disconnected. I also realized that Ralph and I may drift apart. I have to talk to him about keeping his options open, to see other women. Eventually I'm going to tell him, and I don't know how he will take it. As for now, Ralph doesn't want to end it, and I want him to be realistic about a long distance relationship."

Francesca said, "If he wants to have a relationship long distance it's worth a try, then see how things go. Don't give up on him completely, because he could move to Philadelphia to be with you; always keep in touch no matter what."

"You're right; he expresses his love for me all the time. I think I will give our relationship a try, because if we're determined, maybe this would work. Alright Francesca, I'll call you tomorrow."

Happiness with Someone

What does being happy with your mate mean to you? For many couples being happy can mean many different things, and many men and women who are trying to find love are becoming confused about what happiness is when being in a relationship. Happiness with someone can be looking into each other's eyes and knowing that love will always be there no matter what may change in the relationship. Happiness can be listening to what each other have to say without being judgmental towards each other during an argument, and then learning to kiss and make up afterwards. show each other that nothing can come between two people who may disagree on many things. Happiness with someone can also be important when calling each other no matter what time of the day. It's pleasing to hear your mate's voice on the phone to talk about the anticipation of seeing each other at the end of the day. Happiness is accepting imperfection if being with someone who has many annoying or unbearable ways. Even though human beings aren't perfect. Learning to be happy with a person of choice does take time to get used to. Happiness with someone can be complicated sometimes. Getting over difficult times is challenging for two people who want to stay together. Happiness can mean being able to share and not make a big deal out of everything, and knowing the person you're with, isn't someone to give up on completely. Happiness with someone can mean being sexually compatible and loving each other's company. When aging takes over, loving someone shouldn't change. No one can get in between two people in love. Love means making it through thick and thin.

Having Friends of the Opposite Sex

It's always a debatable subject many couples talk about: having friends of the opposite sex. For example, long-term couples do not like it when their mate is continuously being friendly with an ex. Even though there may not be anything going on, and the subject can be a continuous problem. It's natural and healthy to socialize with the opposite sex, but many couples would prefer that friendships with the opposite sex come to a complete stop, when being in a committed relationship. Trust is the main factor to keeping a loving and passionate relationship. The subject can become secretive for many couples starting out. One person could possibly be hearing rumors of something negative about their significant other's relationship with an ex. A strong person who can handle all the difficulties in a relationship can make it through jealousy. If it's a continuous conflict, then it's not meant to be. What matters is a healthy, loving relationship that makes everything complete. Coming together and talking about any difficult issues should be addressed early on, and then try to find a way to get over it. Your mate should know about friends of the opposite sex, because if he or she finds out elsewhere, then it would be as if the subject was a secret. Always know that everyone has friends from their past before they met you, and breaking up that type of relationship should be talked about right away. If you ignore the issue, then trouble will surely begin if not accepting of your mate's ex or friend. If it wasn't the best relationship, keep moving towards the future along with the one you love, because it can be a complicated matter and an uncomfortable situation to be in, if there are no feelings for the person. If there seem to be unsettling feelings, be true to yourself if you think something is there with someone else. Just don't waste anyone's time; be honest and let go of your ex if your mate isn't happy.

Having Something in Common

Wouldn't it be great if every couple could have something in common? Whatever interest men and women share, being able to connect can make the relationship more exciting, because there's always subjects to talk about. Show interest in music, sports, politics, or traveling. Instead of telling your mate I don't have any interest in that subject. Your mate may express not having anything in common, so what should an individual do if not having shared interests? I feel that it's a good idea to show the love of your life that you are trying to be open to new things. Many relationships do have longevity because of conversations about common interest. Life itself has many things going on, and sharing common interest can sometimes keep a loving relationship together. Common interests are important when being with someone you love. Couples who don't have anything in common can enjoy being around friends who share the same interests. Respecting the interests of each other should always be considered, if there isn't anything in common with the one you love.

He Isn't Coming This Way

Many women dress to impress when preparing to meet friends at a social scene. When they finally get there, they will be in a group. They all want to meet a man, but they aren't going to meet a nice man if they're always in a group. Women should separate themselves, or go to the bathroom before going to the club, because a man can be uncomfortable when talking to a woman if she is with a group of friends at all times. There's a good chance he'll approach a woman when she seems to be alone. Men will sometimes keep their distance if a woman does not want to separate from her girlfriends to mingle. Women just standing in a circle throughout the night and consistently going to the bathroom in groups can make a man become disinterested. Some men may talk about how difficult it is to meet someone when attempting to talk to a woman who does not want to separate from her friends, to have a good time or to dance. Some women need to understand that there isn't anything wrong with meeting a man to have a good time, without their girlfriend's constant approval. If a woman is interested in a man when her girlfriends are all standing around socializing, she should think about taking a chance to approach the man who seems to show interest by getting his cell phone number, to call him and make plans to go out. When a woman is ready to go on a date, she'll eventually let her girlfriends know if the man is the one or not. A woman will only wonder what the man would've been like, if she showed interest before the night has ended. Don't have any regrets. Say to your friends, 'You know what? I'm going to talk to this guy coming towards us, because I want to know what he is like.' In today's society, women are becoming bold enough to take the initiative, to introduce themselves to a man they find attractive. So girls, go on and do the same if a man shows interest in you tonight.

He's Sweet, Generous, and Hard-Working

Many women will say to a friend after a couple of dates with a man: "He has all the qualities a woman is looking for! Why isn't he taken?" This is the common question many women will ask about a new man. It feels wonderful for a woman to be with a man who has many qualities women look for. The more time a woman spends with the man she thinks is the one, the more things begin to get serious. Some women may know that there is a problem when it feels too good to be true. Eventually, a woman will assume that the man she is seeing is exclusively hers. As time passes, everything seems to be going well until unexpected circumstances occur, for example, the woman may be in an awkward situation with his female friend. She may confess to the other woman that he is either married or committed in a long-term relationship with her best friend. In time, everything a man has gotten into will be out in the open, for a woman to know more about who he really is. In some cases, it's a possibility that friends of his will be interested in talking to the women and tell her the truth. Many women who find out about a man they thought they'll have for themselves, will then become a shattered thought when another female is in the picture. How would a woman end this type of deception? Some women will continue to date a man who is already taken, and share him with his wife or girlfriend he loves. Women who go through this should talk to a close friend or family member about the situation. Talking about it helps, and a woman can make a conscious decision to end it, because it is the best thing to do. If a woman is going to accept being a part of a man's life, then becoming a happy or unhappy mistress for a while will be her choice, because many women do want a sweet, generous and hard-working man who isn't deceitful. Some women will be in denial and stay with a man who is off limits. If he allows himself to be in a situation with another woman who isn't the love of his life, then he will have to get out of the situation. A man doing this will have to be strong enough to admit to his woman. That she is the only one he loves, instead of leading on his mistress who will become comfortable with the relationship that isn't going to last anyway.

Holly Refrains from Intimacy

Holly is forty-eight years old and lives alone in Worchester, Massachusetts. One summer evening, she decided to invite over her friend Marcela. Holly wanted to talk about some personal matters, so when Marcela finally arrived at Holly's home, they didn't waste any time. Holly said to Marcela, "I think I'm going to refrain from intimacy for a while, because I don't want to continue dating right now. I don't want the emotional connection with anyone, because I've been feeling content in my own world. When I'm involved with someone emotionally and intimately, everything can become complicated, that's why I prefer to wait. I need to focus more on myself because I don't need any interruptions in my life. I don't think that there's anything wrong with waiting for the one. I believe that being intimate with someone I don't intend on marrying can become questionable if the relationship isn't serious. I feel that waiting for that special someone is better than dating just anyone who comes along. My experiences help me decide that I should wait, because I didn't like how I started to feel when I would share my life with someone who didn't want more out of the relationship. I know it's a choice to refrain from intimacy, and I know what's best for me. I didn't enjoy not knowing if the relationship will last, and I don't want a no strings attached relationship. I want to be happy with someone, I feel that this is a choice I had to make."

Marcela interrupted, "Holly, I want you to be happy, but don't let your past relationships affect how you feel about meeting someone who can definitely make you happy. I think there's someone for everyone. I don't want you to give up just to be by yourself. Reconsider spending time with someone, because having a companion is better than being alone. Think about what I'm saying to you."

Holly said once again, "I'm going to take a break from dating to figure out what I really want before I just jump into a relationship."

Marcela replied, "That's understandable; take your time because there isn't no rush."

How to Balance Having a Social Life

Many men and women have a conservative side, and many people have to act conservatively in order to get things done. The stress of daily life can make many people go out to relax and have a good time. People want to have fun, because trying to find a balance can be difficult to have time, to socialize with friends or even to spend time alone. Many men and women are unsociable, and do not know how to act after meeting someone new, due to being isolated because of working all the time. Socialization becomes almost like a new experience, because it isn't easy to balance working and having a good time. There are people who expect to see someone become funny and spontaneous from the beginning, but working hard can sometimes change people. It's difficult to learn how to socialize once again, because life becomes all work and no play. No one wants stress to interfere with having a happy, healthy relationship with someone. It's important in life to find a balance; always include fun and happiness to have a most fulfilling lifestyle.

Is Money More Important to You?

Preston is an independent, twenty-eight year old. He resides in Charlestown, Massachusetts. He's a self-employed, hardworking business man who repairs household appliances. He loves to go to work every day, but he isn't always able to spend time with his wife. When duty calls, he would say to his wife, Nicolette, "Babe, I have to go. I was called to do a job. I know we had plans this Saturday and I'll try to make it back in time to go to see the jazz band tonight. I wouldn't miss out on spending time with you, even though there is a job that has to be done."

Nicolette said, "Alright, I look forward to spending time with you, so please be here on time."

Surprisingly, Preston called later and said, "Hi honey, unfortunately our plans have changed. I can't make it to see the jazz band; another job was lined up for me afterwards."

"What! I thought we were going to spend some time together. I'm disappointed, because I anticipated going out tonight with you," she replied.

"I'm sorry, I have to go and I'll see you later okay." Preston didn't always know what to expect, and Nicolette would understand sometimes. Every now and then she would assume that the opportunities to spend time together were taken away due to Preston trying to succeed financially to provide for them both, even though Nicolette was financially secure because of an inheritance her grandparents left her after they died. They loved her and they didn't want her to worry about money, but she was always waiting for her man's love because he was always worried about money. All Preston wanted was to be a good provider while doing what he loves. Finally, when Preston arrived home, he saw Nicolette sitting in the living room waiting to talk.

When he decided to talk to Nicolette, he said, "I just want to say once again I'm sorry. I promise that I'll be there to spend more time with you, because I do love you, and I don't want you to be disappointed with me."

"I don't want to have a debate about you spending time with me. I don't like to feel that you are more consumed with being worried about money than being with me. Although money is important to have, I just don't want our relationship to be in jeopardy because of it."

Preston replied, "When being in a relationship, there has to be compromise and if there isn't any, a loving relationship will end in disappointment with someone who may feel that money is more important, but that isn't the case with us. There should be some understanding how to work out the situation if I'm always working hard. We have to figure out how to handle things if spending time together doesn't always go as planned."

Nicolette closed with, "Learning how to give and take is important when being together because I do love you too, and if we are in love, then we have to be prepared for the unexpected."

"I understand, Nicolette, and I want you to know that I really do love you and I'll try to spend more time with you as much as possible."

It's All About Respect

If R.E.S.P.E.C.T. is missing, then forget about kissing. Avoid to listen to your mate and constantly guessing and questioning without having any trust. Most people know it's a must to have respect, but let's face it; a person will be instantly unattracted if someone showed a lack of respect and consideration for the other person's feelings. Why do many couples stay in a relationship without respect? Is it for so called love, attention, or just being comfortable with the other person? If respect isn't what you feel that you're getting, then the disrespect will never change for some couples as long as unhappy partners continue as they are. The result is to give repetitive apologies after being disrespectful, and this continuous behavior isn't the answer. There isn't any sincerity in saying I'm sorry, because saying the same thing over and over again can make the relationship progressively worse for many couples. It seems that some couples have to practice and learn how to be in control of their anger. It isn't right to blurt out words that feel good to say in the moment. The pattern of disrespect would creep up to result in loneliness, rejection, and guilt. Couples need to learn to be happy, not become upset and angry. There is nothing wrong with being respectful; if respect doesn't exist in a relationship, then the problem that was endured would eventually make someone turn into a bitter and resentful person. Couples, in general, show their love in many different ways, but if there isn't respect, then no relationship is going to work in the long run.

It's Alright to Talk about Intimacy

When meeting someone new it's important to communicate about intimacy. The subject isn't what many people are comfortable talking about right away, but if there is curiosity, some men and women will talk about it casually over a cup of coffee or go out for dinner. Talking about it beforehand can make a couple understand the likes and dislikes before engaging in such an intimate moment. Many couples who do understand each other intimately will have this conversation at one time or another before or after intimacy. If you refrain from talking about intimacy in the beginning, then the result is a couple being unsatisfied with each other intimately. Communicating from the beginning about the subject is important because men and women do admit that they have unique preferences. Although intimacy is a personal, private moment involving two people. The conversation becomes an uncomfortable and pleasurable curiosity to know about the other person's desires. Many couples do enjoy intimacy and will like to know more information beforehand, instead of waiting to learn about what the other person's desires are. The subject isn't an easy one for many men and women, but it's something two people are going to do often. There is a possibility that many couples will be happy about the outcome after communicating. When couples are satisfied about their intimate moments together, then there shouldn't be any regrets.

Jillian Wanted What Was Best for Herself

Jillian and Kendrick were twenty something year old adults who grew up together in the same neighborhood in Hingham, Massachusetts. They saw each other every day when they were younger and played outdoors as children, but as they got older, they were becoming attracted to each other in high school and college. After a while, they started dating because they grew fond of each other, so they agreed to become exclusive. Eventually, they both became intimate so the thought of leaving each other became harder. They were committed to one another and spent a lot of time together. Surprising, an exciting yet serious matter came about. Jillian said to Kendrick one day, "I'm pregnant." Kendrick asked if she was sure and Jillian said, "Yes, I went to the doctor to confirm the truth, and the doctor said that I was definitely going to be having a baby. We didn't expect that it would happen, I decided that I would like to plan on doing more for the baby."

Kendrick said, "I have to admit that I'm relieved that we completed college before the child was conceived," but Kendrick had dreams of becoming a professional basketball player and Jillian didn't always want to be by her man's side for everything if it involved relocating to another state. When his job became demanding, wherever his team would go, the whole family had to go. It was difficult sometimes for Jillian, but she loved her boyfriend tremendously, so she wanted what was best for her family. Jillian said to Kendrick after his basketball practice one day, "Babe, I'm in this relationship for the long haul. I want to be committed to being there for our family. Although we were not expecting more than one baby, I decided that after the babies are born I'm going to think about what I can do for myself. We both earned a business degree, and I told my parents I wanted to accomplish getting my own jewelry line, because I want to earn my own finances to help contribute to care for our twin girls."

Kendrick replied, "I'm not going to hold you back from what you want to do after helping to raise the girls. I say go for what is best for yourself even though I would rather be the only provider."

After years passed the girls were getting older, Jillian brought up the subject once again to Kendrick. "I'm finally ready to do more."

"Honey, you don't have to feel like you have to ask for my approval, only you would know when you're ready to do what you want."

It wasn't a big deal to her at first because she didn't have a problem sharing with him what was on her mind. They were an extremely close couple and could talk to each other about anything, even though Jillian and Kendrick weren't married. They were always busy moving and traveling because of his career. They were going through so much together that Jillian had invited her sister Juanita over to talk. Jillian said, "I somehow lost myself within the five years of being with Kendrick. I do love him very much and he wants me to do more if I like. Anyway, give me a moment," and then Jillian left to get some snacks and something to drink for her sister. After Jillian left her living room to get a glass of lemonade for Juanita, she started to eavesdrop while Kendrick was speaking on his phone in another room next to the kitchen. She overheard him say that he loved his woman, but he didn't know if marriage was for him. After his conversation, Kendrick entered the kitchen. Jillian said, "I thought we were a family. I hoped that we could get married in the near future."

"I'm sorry. I need some time before deciding on walking down the aisle."

Jillian then returned to the living room with a bewildered look in her eyes and she continued talking to her sister, but she didn't mention what just happened. Then Juanita said to Jillian, "After you came out of the kitchen you looked upset about something."

Jillian told her she'd talk to her another time about it. As more time passed, Jillian soon realized that Kendrick wasn't ever going to marry her, although she'd been there for his every need and helped him fulfill his dreams. Meanwhile, her dreams were on hold to care for her family. She started to think more about what she wanted for herself; she knew that she could be a successful business woman who could have her own jewelry line.

Jillian said to Kendrick one day, "I'm going to take the necessary steps to get there to do what I always wanted to do; I'm going to focus more on me."

Jillian also planned on moving out of the home they had together, because she had to separate herself, so she could think about their relationship. She wanted to have complete independence for a while to begin learning what she really wanted. They both continuously admitted that they will always love each other. Kendrick said once again, "I love you so much, and I agree that we stay apart for a while." Although Jillian figured out what she wanted out of her life, they both knew the twin girls were there number one priority and to always be there for them.

Josephina Found Out the Truth

Josephina is thirty-eight years old and she lives in Chelsea, Massachusetts with her four year old daughter, Shannon. One day, Josephina decided to confide in her friend Rosie about a personal matter she felt she had to reveal. Rosie had no clue what was going on when Josephina invited her over for lady's night on a Saturday evening. When Rosie arrived, Josephina greeted her and gave her a hug. They both sat down on the couch and didn't hesitate to start a conversation. Josephina took a deep breath, "I have something to tell you. I went on a date with someone in the past and we had a one night stand; I actually didn't know him at all. He only told me that his name was Xavier. I gave him my phone number and he would call me often, but I wasn't interested as much as he was. He got the message and eventually the phone calls stopped. As time passed, within a month of ending my intimate encounter, I became very ill. I didn't know what it could've been, but I remember I called you for support. Even though I told you that I was in a relationship with a man you never met at the time, I knew you were always there for me, but I didn't know how to tell you my problem. I figured out there was a possibility that I could've been pregnant with my first child. I didn't want you to know that I had a one night stand, but I felt that I had to finally open up to talk about it."

Rosie replied, "I don't know why you felt like you couldn't tell me; you know we talk about almost anything."

Josephina said, "I was disappointed in myself, and I didn't want you to be upset with me about not knowing the man. After I became pregnant I was in denial for a while, because I knew that the man I slept with the month before could be the potential father of my unborn child. I met him at a party that was held at a night club for a friend I knew for years. He frequented the club on the weekends and I would go to the same place when I felt that I needed to go out, but after a while I would find myself staying home more and more due to being ill; I think I had morning sickness. I finally decided to go see a doctor and he gave me the surprising news that I was pregnant. I was obviously in denial at first, but I didn't tell the man that I knew that he was the father. I was uncomfortable with his reaction. When I did come to the conclusion that I would tell him, I was already five months pregnant. I called him to talk to him about the issue and I thought he would respond negatively, but actually he just listened to what was going on in my life after I became pregnant. It became easier for me to talk to him about how I felt about being pregnant, but Xavier began having doubts about the child being his, so we both agreed on having DNA testing done after the child was born, but during the time I was pregnant, I decided I wouldn't see him. I just kept working at my sales representative job every day. I only wanted to keep busy to get my mind off of the difficulties I got myself into. All I could think about was seeing my new baby; I was extremely anxious every day. Surprisingly, the moment I've been waiting for had arrived, and then it was time to go and get the testing done because the baby was finally born. We reconnected months later and spoke about the matter once again, so I went ahead and scheduled an appointment. The day of the testing, Xavier decided to pick me up so we could go together. As we were driving, we were silent and didn't say much to each other. As we arrived at our destination, we entered the building and walked towards the stairs. We both briefly admitted to each other that we were anxious to know the DNA test results. It was going to be a week or so before finding out the outcome. When everything was said and done after giving all of our information, Xavier and I headed on out of the room to go home. 'Keep in touch after getting the test results,' Xavier said while in the car.

Finally, the day I'd been waiting for arrived. I went to my mailbox feeling curious and anxious after such a long week. I hesitated for a moment then I opened it. The letter read that the man who is mentioned is 99.9% the father of the child. I was happy to finally know the truth, but I didn't call him for a couple of days because I was still shocked by the news; I knew that he will be calling me very soon. When Xavier decided to call he mentioned the letter. Surprisingly, he was actually happy to know that he was the father of a beautiful little girl. He was already prepared to help me to take care of Shannon. Although we never had a serious relationship, we both agreed that caring for our daughter was the only subject we'd communicate about, because doing what we had to do for our daughter was all that mattered to us. Overall, we were happy to find out about the truth."

"That's great that you found out who your daughter's father is. It must have been hard for you, but you should've told me, I thought you trusted me," Rosie replied.

"I do trust you. I was just ashamed so I kept my problem to myself. Next time, I won't keep any secrets to myself."

"That's what I want to hear. I will always be there for you and don't ever feel like you can't come to me. You're my friend and I love you."

Just Looking

When being out and about, many men and women would just look at each other when running important errands. Some people do not intend on meeting anyone standing in line at a grocery store, in a bank, in traffic, or just waiting for the train or the bus. Just a cursory glance without conversation is all many people are comfortable doing; we have the pleasure of looking at attractive people. Some men or women will engage in small talk before getting a telephone number, but the issue of 'just looking' can sometimes cause arguments with couples when being out in public; they take this issue seriously when a stranger is involved who is also attractive. For instance, a man will have an attractive wife or girlfriend by his side, but he would still glance at an attractive woman lustfully. Then, the issue can become a simple misunderstanding that would cause a couple to be mad at each other for having wandering eyes, when the opposite sex is present. On the other hand, some women will also glance at an attractive man, and her husband or boyfriend may become angry if his woman is just looking at another man, but just looking is a natural thing people do every day. Often many couples unknowingly become jealous when witnessing this. It's harmless without physical contact, if you can help it, just pay attention to your mate as much as possible without looking around at someone else, because seeing an attractive person is always a debate when going out in public if there isn't trust in the relationship. Look into the eyes of the person who is the love of your life, then block everyone else out and give your woman or man all the attention he or she deserves, instead of just looking at another person who catches your eye. So if you decide to glance, look rapidly and do not lock eyes if you would like to control the situation without fussing, cursing, and making yourself appear to look foolish in public. You'll draw spectators attention over a subject that isn't worth all the embarrassing drama anyway.

Ladies Night Out

It's beautiful and warm in Washington, DC and it's the weekend. What is the plan this evening for Meagan and Marissa? They have gotten used to staying at home over the years without any fun plans due to being single parents raising a family. However, Meagan called Marissa and asked to go out.

"It sounds like a good idea, and I'm excited to do something fun, but where do two mature, older, single women in their forties make plans to go?" Marissa asked.

"Well, let's go to a neighborhood club, but I do not have any intentions to get wild and obnoxious," Meagan replied.

When they arrived, they showed their identification and entered the club, but they decided to stand against the wall and observe the scene, hoping to have men approach who are around the same age. After some time, they agreed that the men and women all looked so young and vibrant.

"A few men are looking over and glancing; they seem interested," Meagan pointed out.

Surprisingly, an attractive man asked Marissa to dance. After her dance, she told Meagan that the man seemed interested but was too young.

"It isn't easy being a forty something year old woman who is trying to meet someone in a twenty something social scene," Marissa said, "It's like watching our adult children having a good time; meanwhile their mothers are also watching from the side line."

They both had a drink, but did not intend to get drunk. Meagan pointed out that everyone looked as if they are having a more enjoyable time after being intoxicated; standing and watching became more uncomfortable if they weren't also intoxicated.

"We are here to look for a nice man to spend time with." And then Marissa said, "It is funny that people only want to introduce themselves when alcohol is involved. Even though, we decided to give the twenty something scene a try a couple of times, but maybe we should look for another club to go to. We did speak to each other about going to social scenes that are more age appropriate, such as going to places that have jazz, reggae, or blues music. We're getting older and going to a place to have a good time involves a little research to find a club that has good reviews."

Meagan said, "I don't want to have a miserable time and feel out of place because of my age."

A female stranger who was listening to the two women talking recommended a few places for the women to consider going to socialize with people who seem interesting. She mentioned that it's possible that it could be the new social scene to frequent every weekend for enjoyment without feeling out of place.

Leaving Relationships Behind

Many relationships end abruptly due to the lack of interest to try and take the relationship to the next level. The love a man or woman once had is completely over, and many people contemplate leaving. Memories of what were once happier times are all that is left. Many men and women choose to find a new life somewhere else instead of being reminded about the person who would be left behind. Staying with someone who isn't the one can be difficult when making decisions to move ahead. When a couple splits up, the person who is in love more than the other will find it impossible for a while to move on and will deny that it's over over. It's a huge choice to move away as far as possible if the relationship isn't working out. Traveling to a new place would be the time to find someone new elsewhere. No matter where someone lives, start by loving yourself first, before involving a new mate who will make the relationship evolve into love once again.

Love is Questionable

What is love? This is a question people on the journey to finding happiness with someone will ask, but for many, it can become a tiresome search. The chivalry that a person used to have will completely vanish for a while, because no one wants to start over with the introduction, awkward conversation, figuring out what to say, and hoping that it isn't a waste of time to go through a new relationship. All that is associated with dating someone will eventually become difficult if not getting what he or she wants. Usually it takes a mere five minutes to find out a lot about someone. Finding out if it's worth it to continue dating is just an instinct many people experience, and the feeling can be good or bad from the very beginning. Love isn't what many people are getting out of relationships and it is expressed in many ways if it isn't happening. Men and women talk about their feelings openly with a friend to express happiness, hurt, or pain, and many men and women listen to musicians who share their own relatable stories to some extent that may be helpful. Relationships are complicated and people will act out their feelings in different ways, or will give up on love for a while. It's clear that love is something people want, but losing hope in love shouldn't be. As long as men and women are present among each other, they have a chance of finding someone to fall in love with.

Furthermore, love was questionable for a woman named Priscilla because she wanted a lot emotionally from the men who were in her life, but there was one man in particular name Marko who especially found her irresistible. They met at a laundry mat in their Burlington, Massachusetts neighborhood and they dated for a while, but she didn't understand why he loved her so much even though she didn't feel the same way. They did everything together, but Priscilla knew something was missing in their relationship. Yet they were together about five years before she started to fall out of love. Marko found it difficult to move on and Priscilla didn't understand why he couldn't find love with another woman. He was persistent, and one day, Marko saw Priscilla walking home from the grocery store with bags in her hands and he ran up to her to ask, "Why are you trying to avoid me, don't you know that I love you?"

Priscilla said, "I like you but I don't love you; I want you to move on without making things complicated for yourself."

"I'm not giving up that easily, I just want to be with you."

Priscilla said once again, "I told you don't worry about me; find someone who would love you the same."

Marko finally said, "I'll leave you alone for now but I'm not going to stop coming around to see you."

After she ended the relationship completely, he tried to pursue her by telling her spontaneously how he felt whenever he saw her, but she always felt the same. He will continuously stop by her home to talk and she always asked what he wanted, although she knew he would always express his love for her. Year after year, he will continue to see her around town and his eyes would light up like he was viewing a beautiful sunrise that he never seen before. Priscilla will only try to be friends with Marko and it was okay at first, until he started to proposition her for something more, because she ignored him often. She knew the relationship ended, but Marko didn't want to accept rejection, so he became unbearable. She only hoped for Marko to give up on her completely, but he was always unpredictable. So she decided to reach out to her best friend to talk. She wanted to end her friendship with Marko completely, because trying to become only friends wasn't working out.

She said to her friend, "Marko is having difficulties moving on, because he had a hard time seeing me with someone else."

Charlene replied, "He has strong feelings for you and no one else. I suggest that you make plans to sit down with him to talk about what is on your mind. Then he can understand that there isn't anything wrong with being with someone new. Getting over someone takes time, but knowing someone who isn't the person you're supposed to be with. It is hard to accept, when being in denial and obsessed. He just needs to do something to get you off his mind and maybe he can move on. It's the only way to get over a person who isn't in love anymore. I think in time he will eventually get the message, so continue to enjoy your life. I'll be here for you anytime if you need to talk."

"Thank you Charlene. I'll continue doing what I've always been doing in my life. Anyway, I have to go. I'll call you and I'll keep you informed, bye."

Love or Lust?

When seeing someone of interest, many men and women will admit it seemed like love at first sight, but only looking can be lust at first sight, because what a male or female is seeking depends on each individual. If someone is looking for love, then that would be the focus, but if a person is looking for a short-term, intimate encounter, then lust would almost always be expected for people only looking for a good time. Men and women have a personal, acceptable way of meeting someone, when longing for love or lust. Everyone has that same burning desire, to be with someone who is a potential partner to fall in love with or a partner who will accept the lack of commitment that only two people can agree upon. Everyone is looking forward to being with someone, even if it's temporary or long-term, because having good company is something everyone wants to enjoy.

Lynette's Secrecy

A young woman by the name of Lynette was born and raised in Queens, New York. She's a twenty-five year old kindergarten teacher and has been living in her parents' house all her life. She thought it was about time to move out on her own, so she decided to find a new place away from her parents' home. Lynette knew she was going to have a lot more responsibilities, but she felt that it was time to learn how to be more independent, so she found her own place a half an hour away from her parents. She was very pleased with her new apartment.

Up to this point, she has been living alone for three years. She is working hard to keep a roof over her head and keep her finances in order. Lynnette will speak to her parents sometimes and she would tell them that living alone can be draining because she have to be on top of everything daily.
Overall, Lynette let her parents know that she was doing very well for herself, but she was dealing with some skeletons in her closet - personal matters she wasn't proud of disclosing to just anyone, especially to her parents. She decided to contact a close friend to talk about her issues. Lynette was feeling guilty about the deep dark secret she was dealing with and she wanted to talk to her neighborhood friend, Monica, who she trusted.

Lynette invited her over on a Saturday night to talk about the personal matter she had kept to herself for about a year. She started to prepare coffee to sit around her dinner table with Monica. It took a couple of minutes before Lynette decided to open up to talk. She took a sip then looked at Monica with a bit of hesitation.

"Brace yourself for what I'm going to say next. I have been dating a seventeen year old by the name of Joey who is soon to be eighteen. I feel a bit embarrassed about telling you his age, and Joey didn't have an apparent interest to ask me how old I was. We both were in denial for a while about our behavior, but we love spending time together."

"Where did you meet each other?" Monica asked.

"Well, I was instantly attracted to him while at a neighborhood party I was invited to. We had a good time and then, eventually, I became intimate with him. I enjoyed Joey's passion and sexual stamina."

"Wow I didn't know that you liked younger men. Are you sure you know what you're doing?" Monica replied.

"Yes I'm content with him at the moment, but I know it won't last because I'm an older woman. I really wanted you to know that I needed to confess, because my behavior didn't seem normal to me. I felt that it was wrong to date a guy much younger than me. Also, Joey's parents' didn't know about our secret; our relationship became complicated because Joey was always sneaking out his parents' house to see me. I feel guilty and I want our relationship to come to an abrupt end."

After Lynette said all that she wanted to say, Monica replied, "I think you should leave Joey alone before things become too serious for you both. He is too young to be with someone much older. Not to mention what you both are doing could be a problem in Joey's family, especially with all the lies and deception. Lynette, you should consider my advice. You're my friend, and I don't think you're the type of person who would cause turmoil in Joey's family. Your relationship became a deep dark secret that you shouldn't try to repeat again. You will eventually fall in love with someone you truly care about."

Lynette then said, "I appreciate the advice you've given me. I think from now on I will only date men my own age. I know the complications, so I have to get out of this situation with Joey. I do understand that he is young, naive, and only wants an older woman. I have a mandatory rule now, to look the other way when I'm attracted to a younger man. I won't become intimate with a young man who was still in high school, and living with his parents ever again. I know it's just a no-no on my part to allow myself to break a young man's heart."

Marguerite Only Communicated Sometimes

Marguerite is a high school teacher and a busy woman, but from time to time she would call a confidential relationship hotline when she had a minute to spare. She became secretive about her private life and wouldn't usually express her feelings to anyone, she only spoke to a few of her friends. One Saturday night she decided to call the hotline for people who crave relationship advice. The relationship counselor would answer and say, "Hello. This is the confidential relationship hotline."

Marguerite would answer, "Hi my name is Marguerite; I'm a single woman who doesn't always have a lot to do after work. I've been living a double life when I'm alone. I date sometimes and meet people, and then I would call to make arrangements to go out. I had many male friends I could choose from and I do enjoy going out to have a good time, but after a couple of dates, I had a problem calling the men back. They would complain and say that I didn't want to pick up my phone to accept their phone calls. I didn't always have something to say after the date, because I didn't expect anything more than intimacy. Even though, men I've dated always want more conversation. When I was ready to talk, then everything will be fine, but I didn't give them a reason why I didn't want to consistently communicate. I would accept the personal matters in my life. For instance, not having someone to love, and always being alone. I didn't always want to include the men in my personal issues and tell them what I was going through emotionally about what I wanted in a relationship. I had difficulty being with a man if he wasn't what I thought he should be, and they will assume I didn't have any interest in them. Sometimes they will become my friends instead, but I didn't want to talk often to my male friends on the phone, because I felt uncomfortable. They will call to ask me what I've been up to because they hadn't heard from me in a while. I would get over any problems I had in my personal life and then I will give my male friends a call. They liked to continue being friends with me, and expressing only wanting friendship. I will admit to them that I was wrong about not returning their phone calls. I didn't want to lose all of my male friends, even though I wouldn't hear from many of them often. I didn't know that I would lose my male friends and sometimes female friends due to not calling. I will go through so much that I couldn't always let my friends know what was going on in my life; it was too much to talk about. They will assume that I didn't care about their friendship. I'm a private person and I don't tell my friends everything, and I realize that being private all the time wasn't what I wanted, but some of my friends slowly accepted me back into their lives because they truly missed me. So I'm keeping my friends in my life instead of ignoring them."

The relationship counselor said, "It's obvious that you are aware of the difficulties you have when dating, but you have to communicate more often if you do not want to be alone. Being particular is the reason that you're alone; always try to communicate. Make calls to your friends right away and don't wait for days to pass, or else they are going to do the same thing to you when you're ready to talk to them. Treat them how you would like to be treated."

Marguerite replied, "You've given me great advice, and I'll try my best to communicate with my friends more often. Thank you."

Marriage Counseling

Does marriage counseling really work? This is a question many married couples ask. Picking up the pieces isn't always going to work, but if you love someone, working to keep the relationship together is worth a try. Married couples go to counseling for many different reasons to talk about what is ending their marriage such as infidelity, finances, or just having emotional issues relating to falling out of love. Staying together is a lot of work and many couples will try to make it work before giving up. No one enjoys ending a marriage, but it can be bittersweet for couples who want it to end it as soon as possible. Filing for divorce is a sure sign that the relationship is completely over, and standing in front of a judge who will ask the question to confirm it's over. Then a married couple will finally agree or disagree on the decision and they only understand when it's final. Walking away would be the time to accept it, and whatever an individual wants in a marriage will have to be found with someone else who will know what the most important thing in a marriage is. Even though marriage can be complicated, there is hope for everyone looking for love and happiness.

Marriage Ending in Divorce

You've found your soul mate and everything seems to be going great. You're in the beginning stages of learning about each other after getting married and living together. The happiness is there, and it is the start of many things; smiling, always holding hands, cuddling, and the enjoyment of being together intimately is wonderful. Eventually, one child is on the way, then the second, then the third, and it's a big, beautiful happy family, but year after year, the commitment is becoming harder and the happy times aren't the same, and once happier times are diminishing, and the only reason to be together is for the children. As the children get older they will assume that everything is fine. Eventually, both parents will call for a family meeting to reveal the truth to their children. They may not go into detail about everything going on because they do not want to hurt the children's feeling, but what the children are experiencing is obvious; they never wanted to imagine their parents would ever leave each other. Even though the children are now eighteen, nineteen, and twenty years old, they witnessed all that was happening while they were growing up and they would hear the arguments about finances, infidelity, unhappiness, and the lack of communication. A married couple going through this will eventually call it quits and go their separate ways after being together for years. Many married couples put a strain on their marriage because of the joint responsibilities. The result is being stressed out and distant from each, treating each other like roommates. So where does that leave a once happy in love married couple? In some cases, they will reconcile, but many couples will take a trip down to the court house to file for divorce. Nobody wants this to happen, especially if they are supposed to be in love. Marriage ending in divorce happens every day, and the only thing a couple can say to each other is 'I wish you luck, and I hope you have a happy life.' That is such an unexpected ending after being in love, but everyone who is in a relationship or married has to find happiness within themselves before involving anyone else. Finding happiness with someone takes time, and a person will someday find out the truth about what the other person is like. Otherwise, learn to accept what you can and cannot handle about someone who you thought was the one you'd spend your life with.

Mary Gave Raymond a Chance

It was a cold and windy day in Boston, Massachusetts and Mary wanted to take a walk to the nearest convenience store in the evening. She was a single, thirty-five year old woman who has been working hard every day doing some self-employed work over the internet, but she decided to take a break from the computer, to go out and pick up some beverages, for her friends who she invited over for dinner to talk about what they've been going through during the week.

When her friends finally arrived, Mary wanted to share a story about a man she met on the same cold evening. When her friends Jessica and Paula came over they started their conversation. Mary began to express herself.

"When I was preparing to go on a peaceful walk, my intentions were only to get what I needed for dinner, but after arriving at the store to purchase what I wanted. I will then head back to my home and I would take my time in the bitter cold, although I was dressed extremely warm for the weather. I was taking my time because I wasn't in a rush to walk home rapidly; taking a stroll was a breath of fresh air before returning home. When I was only a block away I saw a man at a distance watching me approach the corner where I needed to take a left turn to get home. I saw the man talking to someone outside his vehicle but as I got closer, the man could not take his eyes off of me. I saw the deep seductive stare he gave me but I continued to walk past him slowly without any expectation that he will say something, and when I was crossing the street, the man said goodbye to the person he was talking to and he was looking as if he had the intention to approach me. He spoke loudly to get my attention. At first I wanted to keep walking, but I decided to look back. The man said 'Hey what is your name' and I told him. He said 'I'm not going to hurt you; I just wanted to talk to you. I've never seen you around here before.' I replied with, 'I just moved to this area one month ago.'

I wanted to just go home but the man offered to give me a ride even though I was only going around the corner. I had a slight hesitation to go into his car; it didn't feel right to me but I took my chances because I was turned on by his approach and persistence. When I went into his car he turned on the light inside the car, then he saw my face close up and he told me I was beautiful. The man said that his name was Raymond and he lived in the same area. When I got out of his car to go indoors, he suddenly asked me for my phone number. He also gave me his because he said that he wanted to see me again. I was attracted to his handsome face and his medium muscular build, but I didn't want to get involved with him right away."

Jessica interrupted, "I do think it's a good idea to hold off on being intimate with him."

"I am going to wait," Mary affirmed.

Then Paula said, "Take your time to get to know him first, because if you become disappointed, at least you'll know that you weren't intimate with him."

After a week had gone by, Mary's friends came over to continue where they left off. After her friends arrived, Mary didn't waste any time talking about Raymond again.

"I became involve with him intimately after a week even though I said I would wait. I enjoyed being with Raymond intimately, but overall, there wasn't any chemistry and he didn't have a sense of humor. I will always do all the talking and he wasn't into conversation very much. I gave him a chance, but after being with him numerous times, I wanted to call it quits; he didn't know about how I felt right away, because I continued to be intimate with Raymond on and off."

Jessica said to Mary, "I know what you're putting yourself though; it's important that you're happy with the choice that you made."

"I knew that it was wrong to play games with his emotions. I tried being friends with Raymond at first, but he seemed to want more than friendship. I came to the conclusion to end it but it was difficult. I saw Raymond to tell him it wasn't working out and that I wanted to end being with him intimately. I decided to end it all because I didn't have anything in common with him anyway. When I told Raymond how I felt, he couldn't accept the rejection, so he left my house feeling disappointed. I got myself into this situation, so I'll figure out what to do next."

"If you need to talk about this tomorrow then give me a call, because right now I'm going to be heading home," Paula concluded as Jessica and Paula gave Mary a hug and headed towards the front door.

Things drastically changed and Raymond seemed to have the behavior of a stalker. Mary decided to give her mother Annabelle a call to talk about the matter. When her mother finally answered the phone, Mary confessed, "I was dating a man who I found interesting, but now it's over and he is stalking me. He started driving up next to me in his car out of nowhere to express himself. Everywhere I went Raymond would show up asking me what he did wrong. I would always reply and say the same thing continuously: nothing. It was unusual to me that he couldn't get what I was saying to him. Every time I saw him he was serious with a bizarre facial expression as if something was owed to him. Anyway, I tried to stay calm when I saw him; I didn't express any anger because obviously something wasn't right with Raymond mentally."

"Mary, I hope he will understand eventually but if not, you'll have to consider going to the authorities."

"Mom you're right but that's not what I want to do. I'll come up with my own solution. Ok. Let's just get our minds off of this subject and meet at the mall, because doing some shopping always helps."

Furthermore, Mary called her best friends to tell them that Raymond had changed, and making plans to move forward is the choice, because it had been three years of trying to deal with Raymond's lack of understanding to moving on. Raymond did not know of her plans, only her closest friends Jessica and Paula did. She only wanted her mom to know, but not her dad. It was important to Mary to try and take her time before rushing into any intimate relationships again, especially if there are noticeable signs of unusual behavior, that she doesn't want to deal with in a new relationship with someone. As the saying goes, 'The writing is on the wall.'

Megan's First Love

Megan dated Gerald while they were in high school over twenty years ago and they continued seeing each other after they'd graduated. The relationship that Megan had with Gerald in the past had been a happier time; they were always hanging out together as teenagers do, but Megan wasn't always happy with Gerald because he would do negative things in his neighborhood when being out with his friends. Megan was in love with Gerald and no matter what crazy things he was doing at the time, no one could split them apart. They hung out with friends to go out to eat and to the movies. They just wanted to spend time together enjoying each other's company, and they were only together for a year because Gerald will go in and out of group homes for out of control teens. He needed to learn about consequences, and because of the circumstances, they broke up. Megan couldn't handle Gerald's "running all about behavior" to always hang out with his friends who weren't doing the right things, so Megan eventually moved on and she hadn't seen Gerald in over ten years, but she has always kept in touch with his mother, Beatrice.

Megan matured over the years and she started to talk to Gerald's mother as a friend. Megan's relationship with Gerald was over, but Beatrice was always curious about what Megan had been up to in her life. Megan called one day to tell Beatrice she had been thinking of her.

Beatrice recognized Megan's number, then picked up and said, "How are you doing, Megan? I know you've been busy; I've heard that you were going to college."

"Yes! I wanted you to know that I've gotten my degree; I'm now a dental hygienist. I like what I'm doing, but anyway how are you?"

"I'm doing well and I'm taking one day at a time."

However, Megan didn't ask Beatrice about Gerald when they spoke, but Beatrice started to automatically talk about him because she knew Megan hadn't seen him in over ten years. Megan heard from a mutual friend that Gerald was married but she never wanted to have a conversation about Gerald, which is why she decided she'll only call Beatrice every now and then.

Beatrice continued to say, "I'm now a retired school teacher who has moved to a more suitable environment. I want to invite you to see my new home."

"I would be interested in visiting you at your new home one day," Megan responded.

"I'll be extremely happy if you can make arrangements to finally see me because it has been such a long time."

"I have time off from work on Columbus Day?"

"You're welcome to sit and talk over dinner," Beatrice said, happily.

Megan didn't have any plans so she kept her promise to see Beatrice. When Megan arrived at Beatrice's house the following evening she was very happy to see her and she gave her a great big hug. Beatrice asked Megan to have a seat and they both spent time talking about their lives. Beatrice would speak about her son once again and she wanted to know Megan's thoughts about Gerald's decision to finally get married, and Beatrice asked if Megan wanted to see Gerald's wedding album but Megan wasn't prepared, and she acted as if she didn't know he was married. She was caught off guard when Beatrice wanted to talk about Gerald's new found happiness. Beatrice said Gerald had gotten married about three years ago.

"I really didn't know he was married now, I hope he is finally happy." Megan didn't want to say much more about it but Beatrice desperately wanted Megan to view Gerald's wedding album. Megan noticed how much Gerald has matured physically and how handsome he appeared. His new bride also looked very beautiful. "It's a wonderful thing that Gerald found someone he's happy with and I'm happy for him."

Beatrice said, "I have to admit that Gerald is happily married." Then surprisingly, Beatrice said to Megan, "When you broke up with Gerald he talked about how much he has always loved you, even when you weren't together anymore. He also mentioned this to me even though he was already married."

"He used to be a wild busy body doing crazy things all the time. It's surprising that he is a family man," Megan admitted.

Beatrice was extremely curious to ask Megan if she was ever in love with Gerald. Megan immediately said yes, but not anymore. They both agreed to change the subject, so Beatrice and Megan talked about the enjoyable evening they both had, along with great conversation and a delicious homemade dinner. When Megan decided it was time to go home, Beatrice said that she would call again sometime soon. They once again gave each other a hug and said goodbye.

When Megan got home she had to call her closest friend Latoya who also new Gerald from High School. They started to talk about the visit Megan had with Gerald's mother.

"When I went to see Beatrice I felt awkward talking about Gerald's marriage. Even though, I knew Gerald has changed I feel that I know his past more than his new wife. During the time we were together we'd been through so much. It was also difficult for me to see him in his wedding photos looking so happy with his loving wife."

Then Latoya said, "Gerald was young and he made his share of mistakes but now that he is a mature married man, he probably learned a lot from his past. He decided to change and that's when he found someone he loves. Everyone will understand when it's time to change and settle down after going through trials and tribulations. Gerald learned from his past and now he is a happily married husband and father."

"I realize that your right and even though I'm not married as of yet, I hope someday I'll also walk down the aisle with someone I love."

Mothers-In-Law

Why do so many couples have a hard time with their mothers-in-law? Many people will admit from time to time that their mother-in-law can be controlling and inquisitive. Always interested in knowing if her son or daughter is happy being in a loving relationship. A mother-in-law can have a way of interfering and showing up at the wrong time. She is only looking out for the best interest of her son or daughter, and it can be hard for some mothers-in-law to let go of being in charge of everything, and a mother-in-law can sometimes become overbearing if not being happy about, who her son or daughter chooses to marry. A situation can cause tension if she is not understanding of who her son or daughter chooses to spend time with. A mother-in-law has to know when she needs to accept who her son or daughter is with. Not cooperating could possibly affect everyone involved; it isn't always easy to try and make it work and be a big happy family sometimes, but it's worth a try. Some mothers-in-law just do not want to let go of their son or daughter who wants to start a new happy life. It can be difficult for some mothers to hear their son or daughter admit their in love and are happy. Some mothers-in-law need to consider giving their son or daughter the space they deserve instead of interfering all the time without consideration.

Nathaniel's Addiction to Lora

Lora was going to make dinner for some of her best friends, Melanie and Joslyn. They've been friends since high school and haven't seen each other for about two years. They wanted to spend time together to share stories about their current relationships. Lora started to set the table and she brought out dinner. She prepared Italian food, and she also had red wine to drink. They sat down at the dinner table and Lora wanted to be first to start the conversation about a man she is currently intimate with, Nathaniel. She wanted them to just listen to what was on her mind.

"I have an intimate connection with him. We both enjoy being together, but we usually don't have much to talk about. We only spoke about lust and wanting intimacy, but I feel a sense of emptiness after everything is over. I told Nathaniel that I enjoyed being with him, but we both know that what we have is nothing more than a brief fling. I did pour my heart out and tell Nathaniel that the addiction we have together isn't going anywhere. I know there's very little communication and no emotional connection; it isn't a healthy way that two people should allow themselves to treat each other. So I want out of an unhealthy addictive relationship with Nathaniel but I don't always know what Nathaniel is capable of if we end what we have together. I continue to see him because I feel that he isn't going to leave me alone right away. Nathaniel is extremely persistent and he confesses to me that he would not leave for any reason. I told Nathaniel that it's okay for him to find a new woman. I eventually found out anyway that there were other women involved with him because of his sexual addiction. When I would speak to Nathaniel, he didn't like what was said. He acted as if he didn't like talking to me and he seemed uncomfortable about what I was saying, because I would be honest about his behavior. He didn't want me to tell him what was on my mind all the time about what he was doing, especially when I wasn't around. Nathaniel would sometimes wonder how I knew so much about him without telling him anything. I will express my deepest thoughts about accepting Nathaniel's demands to be there for him whenever he wanted. I'll be there for the sweet brief seduction of his addiction. I feel that I shouldn't give in to him anymore, because going through this just isn't right for me."

Melanie advised, "Getting help to end the addiction is the only way to move on from Nathaniel. Your body is like a temple and allowing someone to treat you this way is going to leave you feeling empty without ever connecting with someone emotionally."

Joslyn added, "Your body isn't a door mat, and you should always know that. You're a diamond and you'll one day find someone who will ask you for a hand in marriage; you just have to be patient. So don't give up on finding someone who will truly love your mind, body, and soul. Just remember that you do have friends in your life. We'll always love you and be there for you no matter what you're going through."

Lora stood up and walked over to her friends and gave them both a hug. "I love you both for being there for me without judging me. Thank you."

No Matter the Circumstances

Isn't it possible that a woman could remain happy even if she decides to be alone without any strings attached? There are many women out there who admit that they cannot be alone and will prefer to be with a man, and there are other women who are married and aren't happy. Many end up pretending they want to stay married no matter the circumstances. Many women would not give up on the fact that having love in their lives is one of the most important things in life. On the other hand, women who became strong after not being successful in their relationship, may have a problem committing; they'll find it hard to continue to make it one of the most important issues in their life, but working hard will be their number one priority for a while until someone new comes along. If a special man eventually becomes part of a woman's life, then hopefully it will work out without all the drama, mayhem, and disappointment. Overall, it's a choice that can become complicated for any man or women with or without a mate.

Oh, She's the Mistress

Women who are seen as a mistress having extramarital affairs prefer to be single because they know that their promiscuous behavior is the reason they aren't married or the type of woman who does not want to hurt anyone. She is intelligent, sexual, charismatic, beautiful, kind, and patience. She has all the qualities many men would find appealing, even though they may already be with another woman. She doesn't take her male relationships seriously, because she only wants him to get to what he really wants. He may be married or single, but she doesn't have any care in the world about the other woman he is involved with. She would not want her man to expose her in any way or get himself into trouble with his wife or girlfriend, and from time to time, the wife or girlfriend will become angry and insecure about her own personal reasons, because many women who are committed to a man don't understand why a mistress would spend time with a man she doesn't have any intentions of falling in love with and who is already taken. A mistress usually wants to be in a committed relationship and is free to do what she wants, whenever she wants, but she may feel empty inside after spending time with a man. She can be a nonchalant woman who isn't looking for trouble. She can be emotionless because she's been in many failed relationships, and now it's a possibility that she's given up on men emotionally. It can be disappointing to her because it's the way she chooses to live her life, although she fools herself into being happy. She will realize that she isn't as youthful as she used to be, and year after year she'll eventually call it quits, because she doesn't want to be a mistress anymore. She wants to reach out to a man to be with long-term. She yearns for so-called love with a man who doesn't see her faults and only recognizes the special individual she really is.

Out of Sight Out of Mind

Hannah and Sergio lived in Chicago where they happened to meet each other at a thirty something bar/club in their neighborhood. They began dating and enjoyed being together until everything started to change; their relationship began to fizzle. They were together on and off for over eight years before Hannah ended the relationship. Although their relationship ended, they had a daughter who they loved and cared for. When Sergio would go and see his thirteen year old daughter, Gabriel, he would always try to get a glimpse of Hannah when she opened her door briefly to allow Gabriel to leave. Hannah will say hello quickly to Sergio and wave goodbye to Gabriel. She preferred to be out of sight after he would arrive at her home sometimes. Hannah always sent her daughter out the door quickly and she didn't always have to express any concerns about Gabriel, but Hannah expressed to Sergio that she only wanted to be friends, even though he wanted more than friendship. Hannah didn't have feelings for Sergio anymore; she knew that she was over him completely.

One day she called her friend Cindy. "I needed to talk to you about Sergio. You know it's a continuous thing for him to see me when he picks up Gabriel; he seems interested in wanting more from me. I feel that it isn't exactly necessary to always see his face, unless he had something to talk about concerning Gabriel. Every now and then he'll walk towards my door to greet me, but I'm not interested in talking to him very much because he seems to assume that we will get back together someday. Also, every time he would bring Gabriel back home we'd have an awkward silence, and I'll make up an excuse to go. Sometimes when he wanted to see Gabriel, I would have my sister Larraine or brother Chas answer the door if they were around, because Sergio always wanted to talk and I'll tell them to keep the conversation short. Anyway, our relationship ended over eight years ago and he continuously acts as if he has trouble letting go. I feel that he believes, as long as we are bonded because of having Gabriel, we should give each other another try, as if there is still something there."

Cindy replied, "You can just wait until Gabriel is a grown up and on her own, you'll deal with him less."

"I didn't expect that I'll be completely over Sergio, but I am. I know that we have to raise our daughter together, and being there for her is the only reason we were tied together after leaving each other. I realize that it's important to be respectful towards him; I didn't want any disagreements about Gabriel. He also appears to be jealous because I was interested in dating other men as time passed. Sergio will continuously express to me that he would always love me no matter what, even if we weren't together anymore. He always tried to pursue me when he felt like the time was right. Sergio said to me one day that he would get over our past relationship in time. After our daughter turns eighteen, I plan on traveling to start a new life to do what I always wanted without Sergio around. I always hear many people say that after having a child with someone; you're tied together forever. Although that is a fact, after the child reaches the age of eighteen. Many couples split and go their separate ways; then seeing each other can be optional."

"After Gabriel becomes an adult," Cindy began, "hopefully Sergio would agree to eventually move on, because doing so is the best choice for both of you."

Hannah replied, "Cindy, thanks for being there because you truly understand what I'm going through."

Pretender

She's a pretender? Acting as if she is associated with certain people who are in a lifestyle she claims to be a part of. She may say she wants a friend who is nice, beautiful, intellectual, and full of life. She knows she is acting like something she isn't. She may be afraid or inquisitive, just because she has a desire most people will frown upon. She is a liberated woman who accepts who she is and knows what she wants. Even though the life she chooses is new to her, she doesn't want to deal with pretenders. Keeping everything she feels to herself is the goal to just wait until she meets someone who isn't a pretender.

Rekindle Your Intimate Desires

The relationship is going well and there are plenty of intimate moments to enjoy. Although, everything may be going great, from time to time the man or woman in the relationship will experience fizzling intimate moments, that becomes less desirable for whatever reason, and then having intimacy will be missing in the relationship completely. A couple may have feelings of depriving each other intimately, so looking elsewhere for pleasure is the only choice. Many couples find it exciting to discover ways of making intimacy more interesting. You need to talk about what can keep the relationship strong instead of ending the relationship because of lack of intimacy. Many couples should take time to make the relationship exciting by being creative and learning different ways to make sparks fly once again. Everyone has different and unique desires and interests, but just remember and reminisce about how the relationship used to be. Don't fall for someone new until working on your most intimate desires with your mate first.

Remembering the First Time Together

Remember when your relationship was sweet as apple pie? You did things like look into each other's eyes and just become hypnotized. Feeling nervous when you don't expect it, and enjoy doing everything together - nothing can break the bond. Everything seems as perfect as a beautiful summers' day. It feels like it will never end and you will love this person forever. Pleasing each other intimately is great, like having a huge piece of delicious chocolate cake, but sometimes it isn't conceivable as to why one person will eventually want to leave. What was once beautiful isn't anymore, then feelings of unhappiness start to surface and you cannot suppress it. Slowly, the love that was there is starting to change. The happiness will be replaced with being distance and silent. You'll no longer look at each other passionately and you prefer to go into the next room or leave, to be alone without your mate's hand to hold. What will happen to intimacy? Most likely that isn't happening anymore; just closing the bedroom door and turning off the lights is the better choice. What will follow when this behavior towards each other happens? There is a sense of fear and regret after leaving that special someone to start over. Many couples ask the question, 'What is love, and do I want to do this again anytime soon?' Many people prefer to wait for a while before being intimate; they would rather be friends first instead of going to bed together too soon.

Respecting Each Other's Time

Sometimes men and women have difficulty making time to see each other. Whether being single, married, or just dating, spending intimate time with their mate can become like a scheduled appointment. Many couples make it work out fine and agree to take their plans seriously. There are also couples or partners who do not seem to be respectful of each other's time, and do not try to have some sort of compromise to make the relationship work. Therefore, some couples won't have a long-term relationship because they're not meeting each other half way to make it work. Most people do have a busy schedule and try to make each other happy. If there is no care about making plans to be together, then eventually there are going to be the constant complaints about not spending time together anymore. It can become a routine to be self-absorbed, not thinking about your mate. Basically, couples who are supposed to be in love can become comfortable together, because many couples do accept that having a busy schedule is a part of life, but communication will resolve many issues. When couples take time out of their day for each other it makes a difference in continuing to have a happy relationship.

Sasha is the Difficult Type

Sasha is the type of woman who would lose her mind for a man, creating scenarios in her head that aren't true. She acts as if she could be wherever he is at all times. Every other woman her man is around is the new woman she assumes he wants. Even if it isn't so, she is the type of woman who will believe it because of all the lies he told about the women he dated in the past; then she became defensive with any woman in her path. If he is involved with a woman for any purpose that may not have anything to do with him cheating, she becomes angry easily. For example, if he is fixing a broken washing machine for a female friend or if he is seen hugging a woman from the past he hasn't seen in years, she will then assume he would start dating them. Over a period of time, all of her negative experiences with other women made her become controlling, obsessed, and mentally unstable because she loved him so much. When women try to pursue him, she believes that she can stop him from his sexual addiction. As always, every woman she sees is the next target and she'll be waiting to express her unstable thoughts, which could be false, just out of jealousy. The thought of her man always being with another woman makes her lose her mind continuously. Her so-called 'love' is beyond what her man can handle, but he stays with her anyway. He loves her but his cheating made her become another person she didn't know she will be. He loves the attention sometimes and he wants to leave her, but admits he doesn't want to be alone because she is all he has. Being in love is her addiction, so she will speak loudly to any woman if she has to.

This is love for many men and women, and only time will tell if the connection would last, because if this type of relationship takes place, there isn't anything happening but mental abuse, pain, fear, and unhappiness. A couple going through this can take years to leave each other; it isn't a choice for many men and women to leave a situation like this one. Only a clear mind can understand what to do next, because a clouded mind thinks this is love when it truly isn't.

Secret Intimacy

Nicolette and Cullen met at work, and they managed a company in China. After meeting, eventually they got married and moved to Fitchburg, Massachusetts. They had two sons, Lionel and Clyde, and everything seemed to be going well, but as years passed, their relationship began to fizzle. After twenty years, they weren't communicating much anymore and they would find themselves keeping busy to avoid disagreements when they were around each other. They loved each other, although their relationship wasn't the way it used to be. They tried to make their relationship work for the boys, but they were getting older, now fifteen and seventeen years old, and because of the boys' ages, Nicolette and Cullen came to a mutual agreement to file for divorce.

Lionel and Clyde decided that they wanted to continue to live with their Dad instead. Nicolette was content with the decision made. They thought it was best to get a divorce and move forward. As time passed, they started to date and meet other people. Surprisingly, once they moved on, they started to miss each other dearly and will occasionally call to talk. Nicolette thought it was a good idea to tell her mother what was going on in her personal life. Nicolette prepared a cup of coffee for her mom and they both sat. She took a deep breath.

"Mom I need to talk to you about an issue I'm concerned about. I called Cullen last week to ask if he was seeing anyone. He said that he happens to be seeing someone new, and I also told him that I was seeing someone too, but I miss him a lot. Mom, although we are divorced, we have interacted inappropriately. We would meet each other secretly and become intimate. We knew that it was awkward to be together once again, and even though we both had someone else, we only wanted to be together because of the happy memories we once shared. Now we're holding on to a secret, from the new people in our lives. We didn't want to get back together, but we were dishonest towards the companions we chose. Cullen and I didn't speak to each other after being intimate; we didn't want to destroy our loving relationships."

"Nicolette I'm disappointed in you. You went through a difficult divorce with your husband, not to mention the emotional pain Lionel and Clyde had to deal with. I suggest you don't tell your kids about this. You and Cullen are adults, but you both are being selfish because of the people involved who have no idea about what's going on. Think about your choices and try not to hurt anyone, especially yourself.

Nicolette knew she was right. "I'm sorry I disappointed you mom, but I'm going to be fair and make the right choice."

In conclusion, Nicolette and Cullen kept their intimate relationship private for years. They continued to live a normal life with their mates whom they were committed to. Everything started going great for both of them and they didn't tell their partners about their secret. They decided that ending everything completely was the best choice. They had a conversation one last time to see if they made a mistake about leaving each other, but they both were very happy about the new people in their lives. They didn't say anything to their mates, because they didn't feel that it was necessary. Only her mom Roseanna knew, but no one else found out about the intimate moments they shared together. Nicolette and Cullen did admit to each other that the truth would have exposed a negative outcome, so they decided that moving on from the past and staying apart was their choice.

She is an Urban Soldier

She is always on a mission alone like a soldier. She holds her head up high. No one can effect what she thinks about herself, but she's been hurt by many men and doesn't have an interest in putting up with anything new that comes along. That's why she is a soldier, wanting love and her freedom, but only having survival on her mind and focusing on what is going on in her life every day. She is a soldier, changing her style from dressing like a lady to wearing what she feels comfortable in. Wearing her soldier boots, jeans, sunglasses, and her female fitted black cap for what is appropriate for only running around in the streets and working hard to help herself without looking for the attraction of men. She is a soldier, having control of her own life. She doesn't accept everything people say to her. Especially when trying to keep men at a distance to get her priorities in order without them controlling her destiny. She is a soldier, not only thinking of herself, because she always put her family first. Even though she wants a man to love her, she does want more from a relationship. She doesn't give into the constant yearning desire of men; she knows when it's the right time to be with someone, only doing what she knows is best after turning her life around to continue on the journey to understand who she is. Eventually, she wants a beautiful person to share her life with, to only have happiness and fulfillment.

Shelly's Abrupt Ending from Troy

Shelly is a woman who didn't spend her youth partying. Her parents were very strict with her and she lived with them in South Carolina until she was twenty-five. She decided to search for her own place, and she would speak to her friend Shawna about wanting to party more often after moving out of her parents' home. Shelly felt that she needed more freedom. Shawna agreed it was definitely time for her to move out of her parents' house. After a while, living with parents can sometimes become difficult because you can't do whatever you want to.

Shelly said, "It is going to be a big transition to move out but I think I can do it."

After a month, Shelly eventually found a new place and she was excited that she could finally be on her own without her parents' involvement all the time. Eventually, Shelly would invite her friend over to talk about having more of a social life and about dating. When Shawna came over to visit, Shelly said, "I know I have my own place now and I'm excited, but I don't want to move too fast, let's just go out to celebrate my accomplishments.

Shawna agreed, "That sounds like a great idea, because our lives are all work and no play."

Shelly requested, "We should go out on Saturdays because I haven't gone out recently and I think that's what I've needed."

When they went out the following Saturday, Shelly met a nice young man while having a great time at a club in their neighborhood. Shawna and Shelly were standing around when a handsome man asked Shelly to have a drink. Shawna said, go and mingle because he looked interested.

"He does appear to possibly be a nice man. I'll go have a conversation with him."

When Shelly started talking to the man, she noticed that he didn't speak very much. Shelly found herself doing most of the talking when they talked about life.

The music was very loud, so Shelly told him if they exchanged phone numbers, then she'd give him a call another day. He said that's fine and told her his name was Troy. They both agreed that they'd just keep in touch and decided to go back to their friends.

Shelly said to Shawna, "I would like to date him; I do hope that we can have a long lasting friendship. I will consider going out with him next weekend to go dancing." Shawna hoped he could be the one for her.

The following weekend Shelly called Shawna to talk about the date. As the phone rang, Shelly anxiously wanted Shawna to answer. When she picked up her cell phone she said, "I want to talk to you about how my date went last night with Troy. We had a good time, but after we left the club he still didn't have much to say. He is also looking for something more. I'm going to consider being with him intimately."

"Are you sure?" Shawna asked.

"Yes, I haven't been with anyone for over a year. I also need friendship and conversation but I haven't been getting that from him so far. I think I'm going to consider calling it quits if he isn't going to open up to speak more often."

Shawna pointed out, "It's going to be difficult for him to end everything because he seems to like you."

"I know, but I'm going to definitely have to tell him it's over, or maybe I just won't call him again."

"I think you should be careful what you say to him. I hope it doesn't turn out to be a big misunderstanding."

"I think everything will be fine," Shelly hoped.

Troy stopped getting phone calls from Shelly so he started calling her continuously, but she didn't pick up the phone when he would call. One day he decided to show up uninvited at her doorstep. She didn't like it and she told him that she was busy. Troy said he wanted to continue to see her, but Shelly said she would give him a call when she's ready to go out again. When he was gone, Shelly had to call Shawna once again about what has happened.

"You know what? I have no intentions to go out with Troy again. I'm just going to end it completely although I said I'd call him."

"It seems that he has a hard time ending whatever he thought he had with you," Shawna noticed.

"I was only intimate with him one time and now he thinks we have a relationship. Maybe he will give up after a while because I don't want to waste his time, but we'll see how everything goes."

Weeks had gone by after Shelly met Troy at the club and he eventually got the message. She was lucky that it ended the way it did, because after she realized he wasn't the one for her, she only wanted to have a good time and nothing more. Sometimes when she dated someone new, things didn't go the way she planned, then Shelly knew that the search for a good male companion have to continue.

Silent Resentment and Anger

When your mate walks through the front door after work, sometimes you can look into his or her eyes and see a different facial expression. Only when looking into each other's eyes can you tell that something is upsetting your mate. In some cases, silence, resentment and anger is associated with a problem that's kept internally. A once happy couple will have issues that involve communication when there is tension causing unhappiness. Then having a discussion will be the time to open up and share whatever it may be, because silent resentment and anger can only get worse for the person having these feelings. This is one of the first signs of losing trust in the person you thought you knew, and just being silent, resentful, and angry is an unhappy way to live. So communicate as much as possible about what is on your mind.

Sitting and Looking Beautiful

It's a hot night in Southern California and it's time for Tina to get ready to go to the club with her girlfriends, Lacy, Fancy, and Peaches. Tina searched for the most fierce outfit, and getting all the accessories needed to prepare to look great. Tina was interested in going out because she wanted to look for a man. After getting ready, her girlfriend Lacy called to say she was on her way. In the meantime, all the girls would meet at the club. When Lacy arrived at Tina's house she rang the doorbell. Tina answered the door and Lacy told her she looked great.

"You're looking wonderful for your night out with the girls. Come on, get your things and let's go and meet them all there."

Tina spoke to Lacy in the car about the hope of finding a man. Overall, she just wanted to enjoy her night. When Tina and Lacy arrived to greet their other friends at the club. They were checking out each other's beautiful clothing. This was a problem with Tina; she planned on having a good time with men but all her girlfriends wanted to sit and look beautiful and just have conversation with each other. After a lot of conversation, Tina wanted a man to dance with her, but her girlfriends had a lot on their minds about what was going on in their lives.

Tina said to Lacy, "I feel like I'm just sitting and looking beautiful, and this shouldn't be what our night is all about. Men are interested, but I see that they're beginning to lose interest. They are looking from a distance at us, but they see that the other girls' facial expressions are focused."

Lacy looked around. "You're right, the men are looking disinterested."

Tina said to Lacy, "While they're talking, I'm going to have a good time. Realistically, I know I'm going to make the best out of my night. I'm going to drift away from our friends for a while to dance with a man. I'd like to enjoy a drink with a man who will find me attractive in my gorgeous outfit. Right now, only a man's comment would matter more than my girlfriends."

Lacy said "Tina it's your choice to go right ahead to have a good time. You don't have to stay with us, but it's also your choice if you want to spend time with your girlfriends tonight."

"You know what? Even though you're right about me doing what I prefer to do, I feel like I should stay with my friends tonight."

Tina decided to observe men from a distance because it was her choice to do so although her girlfriends' needs were to dress to impress and console each other about what was going on in their lives. They mentioned their behavior after separating for the night. They all agreed that they will have a better time in the future to dance, laugh, and just have a good time. Instead of choosing to sit and look beautiful and worry about their everyday lives.

Starting Over

Many men and women are afraid to start over in relationships because they don't want to give up on love. Starting over isn't something men and women want to talk about often until it happens. Whatever causes someone to slowly lose interest isn't something anyone can control. If it's meant to be or not, looking forward to being with someone without losing interest is unpredictable, and most people don't see it coming. It's okay for men and women to look forward to starting over. Many people expect that being in a relationship is preferred, even if it's for a short time. Having a relationship last as long as possible is the desire, and many people are fascinated with starting over, because finding someone is wonderful. People will agree, that only enjoying love while it lasts is expected, but can be challenging when being with someone. Only an individual can figure out where the relationship is going.

Sybil Didn't Want to Hear It

What's a woman to do when everyone is telling her to wake up because he isn't for you? Her family and friends tell her that she can do better. Her name is Sybil and she is a thirty year old woman who is intelligent, friendly, kind, and well educated, but she has a man by the name of Oliver who isn't the kind of person who contributes to helping his family. They have a ten month old baby boy named Adrian, and they love each other dearly, but Sybil has to work because her man doesn't have any luck in holding down a job. Their friends and family always noticed that she will do more for the family. They'd continuously tell her that he wasn't the one. Sybil will get angry with anyone who will say anything about her man because she just didn't want to hear it. Sometimes she will immediately end relationships with anyone who is willing to talk about her man. She'll call her best friend Leda to talk about what she was dealing with and it wasn't an easy situation, because her mother, Peggy, was living with her for a while. She'll see her daughter and her grandson needed assistance in their household. Oliver wasn't stepping up to assist Sybil with anything; he will only do what he wanted to do, such as spending time during the day drinking and going out with friends who weren't doing much with their lives. Sybil only wanted Oliver to help with his son. She will also complain about all the domestic work, she would do without any of his help, and Sybil will always call Leda to complain.

"I want things to change because what Oliver is doing isn't acceptable to me. First of all he sleeps all day, and when I get home from work he would leave because he didn't always want to hear what I had to say. It's like taking care of a child."

Peggy overheard her daughter talking to her friend about her personal matters. Peggy decided to intervene and say, "What can I do to help with your situation?"

After getting off her cell phone, she continued to listen to her mother but once again, Sybil just didn't want to hear it because it became upsetting for them both. After Peggy stayed to talk about her daughter's situation, but Peggy didn't want to be around if Oliver was home. Peggy knew it was hard for her daughter because she didn't want to be alone. "I can't pick and choose your mate, but I'll tell you what, you'll always be my daughter and I think you deserve the best. If you can't see what is going on right now, then I hope eventually you will and can learn from this."

Sybil interrupted and said, "I love him, and he loves me and his son. That's all that matters right now."

"Okay, but I'm still here for you no matter what. I'll just stay out of it," Peggy said as she walked away to sit in the living room to watch television.

The following day she called Leda again to talk about the conversation she had with her mother. Sybil wanted to share how she felt about her mother and the problems surrounding Oliver.

Leda told her, "Every person chooses who they will fall in love with. You're not in the most perfect situation, and only you can make a choice whether to stay or go."

"I wish my mother and my other family members would just let me live my life. I can choose what I want to do when it's time."

"Yes you're right, and if you do not want me to interfere anymore, I won't because I will always want to be your friend."

"You're at least the only one who isn't judging my situation. I know for sure that you are someone I can talk to," Sybil concluded.

The Emotional Replay

Many people do not think before jumping into a relationship with someone intimately. Many men and women will talk about the emotional connection to someone who they will have strong feelings for, and sometimes the feeling of being attached to someone can occur too soon when being involved. The good memories aren't easily forgotten for many people who talk about the past and present and could not let go of someone emotionally. The happier times aren't always easy to reminisce about, especially when seeing the person who was thought to be that special someone. It can be a sudden coincidence to see that person in public. Sometimes there is the possibility of two people reuniting to continue having a relationship. Sadly, if the relationship didn't work, then it isn't a good idea to reconcile. Most men and women understand why they left in the first place, and some couples who were in love give each other another try again and again, because the emotional connection was unforgettable. Therefore, reminiscing about how it used to be can be the reason many couples eventually remain together, due to a strong emotional connection. On the other hand, if two people haven't treated each other with respect to improve the relationship, then there shouldn't be any reason to reconcile the relationship whatsoever. In conclusion, most people can become vulnerable with someone they once loved and making the decision to go back to being in the relationship may or may not be the right choice. Communicating and being honest with each other is the only way to know if starting over is worth another try.

The Flirtation Isn't Going Anywhere

Clayton and Jocelyn are neighbors in the same building in New Bedford, Massachusetts. He is fifty years old and she is thirty five. Every day Jocelyn sees Clayton outside in front of their apartment building, and she'll watch him get prepared to enter his car to go to work. Usually, Jocelyn watched his routine as he goes in and out of his apartment. They greet each other every morning for a long period of time. As the years passed, Clayton started flirting with Jocelyn, engaging in small talk, smiling, and enjoying brief conversations before he went in or left his apartment. They watched each other for three years, but the flirtation lasted for about a year. She eventually wanted the neighbor to say more because she was interested. She also loved his foreign accent; he was from the Caribbean Islands. She assumed something would happen because the flirtation continued every day when they saw each other.

Jocelyn called her mother Barbara one day to talk about Clayton again. "I find him interesting, but I don't think he is ever going to ask me out. As time passes, my presence becomes less visible for him to see, because I choose to avoid him. I didn't want to continue flirting with someone who wasn't going to say what he really wanted. I knew that Clayton was interested, but I couldn't understand why he didn't say a lot more, such as being bold enough to ask me to go out on a date. I don't see him with anyone, but it seems, he actually never had any intentions to ask. As long as I saw Clayton, I never saw him with a woman. That's why I would assume that he was interested, and I would only wait until he said what was on his mind first before I spoke. As time continued to pass, I will only get to know him by small talk. We have gotten to know each other and we passed the uncomfortable introduction phase. I waited for something to happen but nothing ever did, so I continue to avoid him. Clayton never said what he really wanted and all I did was flirt, just waiting for him to make the first move. He rarely sees me and he will miss me. I knew this because I'll take a peek out of my window when I heard his car in front of the building. When he gets out of the car, the huge smile he once had, after seeing me is no longer. I will see him out my window, and Clayton wasn't aware that I was watching him. He didn't smile as much as he used to, and when I did see him outside, I acted as if he was a new neighbor I recently met, but I continue to live the single life and all we said to each other was 'good morning' and 'hi' nothing more."

Her mother answered with, "You know I always said to you if things doesn't work out. There are always more fish in the sea, so continue to keep your eyes open for someone you find interesting, because dating doesn't stop with Clayton."

They're Over Ninety and Still Together

Look at those two, they're over ninety years old and they seem to be a happily married couple, still looking at each other passionately. It's so beautiful to see happy couples growing old together and walking, holding each other's hands without a care in the world, just enjoying a sweet kiss on the lips. They still enjoyed each other's company; until death do they part, and they will not show signs of slowing down any time soon. Anyone watching would imagine being in love just as long as an elderly couple. A person may want to ask 'How many years have you two been married? And what is the secret of a successful marriage?' Watching a happy elderly couple in love, is obvious that people can still be in love for many years and have pleasure being together in public. Anyone who has been in love before, will know for sure when looking at a ninety year old couple. Throughout the years they've been together, it has a lot to do with give and take. Watching two people succeed in a long-term commitment is wonderful. Many elderly couples do know each other and they know how to fulfill their needs when no else could. Many people want to live happily married as long as possible, and observing the elderly couples today, gives many people hope. Anyone wanting to see two people in love can learn a lot from a happy elderly couple, showing their love for each other in public.

There They Go Again

There they go again those two best friends looking for the one. They'll ask that common question, women usually want to know before going out on a Saturday night. Who is he going to be tonight? Is he going to be young, middle aged, or an elderly man? Women who go through this do not know what to expect. They become disappointed when trying to look for someone to spend time with, but will only go home alone and try once again next weekend. Women don't want to seem desperate, but many do. Even though they go out to have a good time, sometimes the night may include unexpected situations. Such as getting involved with someone the first night or making plans to go out another time with the new man of interest. Sometimes, best friends who do have difficulties finding a new man will know it's the first move that matters and they need to be more open to trying the awkward approach, which may or may not result in rejection. Even though women do become frustrated about dating, they don't give up on men completely. Women may talk about meeting a man of choice and can sometimes feel hopeless when trying to find a man to date, but they'll continue to have a good time without trying too hard to find someone new.

They Call Them Cougars

It isn't common to see older woman with a younger man, usually it is the other way around. Living in this day and age, older women are looking better. They're more experienced and content with themselves. Many mature women will have help from cosmetic surgeries, Botox, and working out every day with a good diet regiment. Younger men seem to be interested in older women in today's society, and there are people who created a word for older women going out with younger men - they call them cougars. Many older women are well rounded and know what they want. A younger man is attracted to a woman who is extremely mature and established, but as an older woman continues her relationship with a younger man. Then over time her life becomes complicated because some younger men can be reminded of qualities his mother possesses. This isn't what a younger man or an older woman wants, but it does happen in some cougar relationships. Many older women do try to treat their younger man as if he is close to her own age without continuously reminding him that he is too young, and there are some men who always enjoy pleasing their woman, and would only be there for his woman's every need. As time goes on, a younger man may consider going out with someone his own age because he may feel that he is missing out on something with a younger woman. Many younger men will stray eventually if their only priority was to look for a good time with an older woman. Whatever a man prefers when it comes to an older woman, it can be a new experience. There isn't anything wrong with trying to find exciting company to spice up an average love life, because it's fun to try new things that haven't been done in relationships before. Whether you're a cougar or a young, handsome stud. It's okay to find someone to love and have fun with. We only live once so if the opportunity is there, go for it!

Trent Craved Marital Advice

The guilt started to slowly approach for Trent; he is a forty year old man who has been with his wife Paulette for over ten years in Malibu, California. Anyway, Trent was insecure, controlling and jealous. He didn't trust his woman because of the thoughts he consumed for seeing other women. He loved his wife and children, Gavin eight and Tessa five years old, but he didn't have any control over the desire to be with other women he found attractive. Trent would have conversations with his brother Owen, and when he came home, he talk about another woman he was seeing. Trent will speak to his brother and ask him for advice about many things, but he didn't talk much about what was happening in his marriage. He was a private person who kept his relationship personal. There weren't any conversations that Trent had with his brother in the past about marital issues, that were problematic. Such as being possessive and following Paulette around to see if she was with someone else.

Trent said to his brother, "If my wife decided to see someone else, I will go insane. I don't think I would accept her dishonesty."

"You don't want your wife to cheat so why are you doing it?"

"I actually don't know why. I don't have a clear understanding, why I enjoyed being with other women while I was still married."

Owen said, "Being married isn't easy, but you shouldn't do things to others that you wouldn't accept being done to you, and you're doing all the wrong things you don't want your wife to do."

"Owen your right, and I'm going to try to consider being faithful to Paulette, and maybe I wouldn't feel guilty anymore. Only I know what I'm doing and no one else."

"Well you need to work it out soon. You don't want her to leave you just because you couldn't control your desire for other women," Owen warned.

"She is being told by her friends and family to leave me, but I do love her and my children very much, and I'm going to prevent that from happening. I don't think that I will find someone like her who would deal with my type of behavior," Trent confessed.

"Work things out with her and tell her how much you love her and the children. Admit that you were wrong and maybe she will accept what you said. Paulette may try to make things work, especially for the children's sake. Think about what you're doing, and if the way you're behaving is worth it."

Wanting Intimacy

Many men and women do have an extremely busy lifestyle due to working, taking classes, or raising a family. When there are many distractions every day, couples rarely have any time and will become less interested in intimacy. The stress of doing other things in life can make it difficult for people to enjoy intimacy as much as they used to. As a result, many men and women would prefer to date without any strings attached, because of their everyday lifestyles. In some cases, many men and women will decide to be alone for a while because of a previous failed relationship and only look for intimate encounters, nothing more. Many people come out of relationships unhappy and bitter. Then they'll take time to be with someone new again. Until the yearning desire for someone to be intimate with arises to fulfill the lost feelings, even if there isn't a love connection. But realistically, many people want to be with someone to grow old with and when it's time to find that special person to be close to, and possibly be the perfect person to fall deeply in love with. A relationship can be wonderful with someone who can always be there to make it last as long as possible.

Wanting the Whole Package

An emotional and physical connection is wonderful if found in one person, but many people in relationships do not get what they want from just one person. It can be one of the many reasons people cheat. A physical or emotional attraction isn't always there for every man and woman, so looking elsewhere is what many people choose to do, and some people want their significant other to have it all, such as wanting someone who is funny, charismatic, articulate, and a romantic person who makes plans to do something wonderful and out of the ordinary. Many people need to learn about their mate, so they can make a choice to accept or reject someone and to know what is worth working on or not. In many relationships, when married couples are together over thirty years, many of them will mention continuously that being married isn't easy and there is a lot of give and take when being in love with someone. Whatever an individual is looking for, a complete package shouldn't be the expectation because we've all heard the saying 'No one is perfect.' We are slowly accepting that everything isn't going to be found in one person, so accepting people for who they are is usually what we should look forward to from the beginning, not perfection.

What is Your Dating Introduction?

When some men are attracted to women they may be uncomfortable introducing themselves, resulting in an awkward stare or stammer. A woman may not always know when a man is interested in her because he may not know what to say, therefore a woman may not have any idea a man is attracted to her. He will lose out on meeting someone new because he didn't know how to introduce himself to a woman, and there are some men who have difficulty thinking about what to say past the first sentence. They will give up, and will become speechless, then walk away. When some men start a conversation, they would wait for the woman to share what she is going through in her life, but a man never knows what to expect, whether it's her happiest or saddest thoughts. The outcome is always unpredictable; it's the most anxious situation to be in. People take their chances to find someone they think is special, because dating a new person will always start with an uncomfortable introduction. Couples remember meeting for the first time and enjoy speaking to family and friends about their first date. Usually it's a unique, memorable, and a happy moment that is cherished. People can become uneasy to think about starting over with anyone, and will take some time from doing so, but don't lose hope. Having some idea of what to say before engaging in a conversation is best, because it's easy to lose the attention of the person of interest if not knowing what to say. Having confidence, a nice smile, and being bold enough to go after what he or she wants is helpful, but be prepared to possibly be rejected. If this does happen, continue to be happy; don't become discouraged because it's okay to try again. After a while speaking is easier, so don't become a person who prefers to be alone rather than to meet new people, because of an uncomfortable introduction.

When Your Intimacy isn't Private Anymore

Many people admit that they enjoy the pleasure of having their relationship private, but whether being a celebrity in the public eye or just an average person in an average intimate relationship, it can be difficult to keep private. Some people can become inquisitive, especially family and friends who want to know about the intimate details about relationships. Many share their fun and exciting adventures with loved ones, but what a person does intimately is private, because talking about intimate, private moments openly with just anyone doesn't lead to having a happy and fulfilling relationship. Consequently, what a couple does in the bedroom should be personal. If not there's a possibility that having a confrontation or disagreement will happen. Even though being intimate is exciting, it feels good to just keep personal thoughts between two people, but being free to express sexual desires is the choice for many people who will seek for someone special, and also to have a conversation. Especially in these times. Many people are seeking love interests from online dating sites, but there isn't anything wrong with doing so. Many relationships these days are developing in cyber space, but there can be reluctance to meet someone in person. Most men and women do whatever they want anyway when privacy is concern.

Why Complain, Isn't Your Husband Working?

As they grow up into womanhood. Many women admit that having a beautiful wedding, and to eventually live in a home with the white picket fence is the ultimate dream, but we all know that so much has to happen in between and everything in life takes time, whether it's planning the wedding or purchasing a first home. Many things married couples work for usually take time to accomplish after the wedding. They continue to work their day job to enjoy living as newlyweds, but sometimes married women complain about their husbands never being home because they're always working, and many women do decide to work every day, but complaining about their husbands is common; it's a big subject in many marriages. They talk about having feelings of emptiness as if they were never married, and they complain about doing mostly everything such as taking care of the finances, domestic work, or caring for the entire family. Even though many husbands aren't always present, their wives want to know that they're in a relationship with someone, instead of feeling as though they're in a marriage alone. Many women need to face the reality that most men are determined to work hard and to have their husband around often is merely impossible. Especially, if you want to be with someone who is an ambitious provider. Don't complain; make plans to figure out what days would be a good time to spend with your husband. Complaining isn't the answer, because most people have to work to survive.

Wife, Mother, or Girlfriend

Women go into relationships with men, and wouldn't know what to expect at all, and after getting to know the new man. He will be interested in a wife, mother, or girlfriend all wrapped up in one. Women are looking for more than just that. They want a man who knows what he wants and doesn't expect a woman to be in charge of everything. Couples should always work together and understand what the other wants. On the other hand, knowing what's also important, because people want to be in a relationship with someone who also has skills: Such as cooking, cleaning, and doing the laundry. Strong women do not accept doing everything without having assistance from their significant other. It is wonderful when both people have control over what they want when getting involved so working together is easier, because having longevity, love, and friendship will be satisfactory for a woman who knows her role. A woman shouldn't be the one to feel confused about playing three roles as a wife, mother, or girlfriend in the relationship. Women and men want someone who is passionate and independent. Without question, couples should know their role and try to make the relationship work. It isn't easy to always figure out what will keep a relationship intact, but it's important to say what you're all about and what you want from the very beginning before wasting someone's time.

Yearning for Your Husband's Presence

You've met the man of your dreams and he's all that you desired, but after the wedding "everything" isn't what you hoped it will be. All your friends and family have started to notice that although you're happy with the love of your life, he is busy working in the armed forces and isn't going to be around as much as you thought he would. All the attention from friends and family is exciting before being married, but many women will express that being married is similar to being a single mother, and the feeling of loneliness becomes difficult. It's also important to make friends wherever he goes, but he loves his family and he will just continue living his life, but will miss out on many things with his family. All a woman can depend on is social media, letters, or talk on the phone, about when he can see his family. Every now and then a family member may ask, 'Aren't you lonely when your husband is gone?' Then, a loving wife would usually be positive about her husband's absence, because he is pursuing his dreams and providing for his family's future. This is the life many women are familiar with, but to accept not seeing each other every day is extremely difficult. Men will have to plan to sit down with his wife, and figure out what she really wants. Communication will involve making choices to try and make it work. Understanding all aspects of what is involved, but becoming disappointed will happen sometimes, because it's a choice to make it through happy and difficult times. Women who are in love will try and make it work out, but on the other hand, there are women who may decide that it's time to leave the marriage. Some women will divorce a man who is in the armed forces, law enforcement, or an athlete. If a woman is strong enough and patient, then she should be by her man's side no matter what. That's what love is all about; trying to find happiness together is all two people have, when going through this complicated life changes such as this one.

You Can't Force Someone to Love You

Relationships aren't guaranteed to be long term for many couples, but they continue to try and make it work. Everything starts off well and then things slowly change. Nobody knows exactly what will make a relationship change rapidly and only if both people who are involved can make it better, and decide if it's worth keeping the relationship together. However, there could be one person in the relationship who calls it quits and has no interest in making it work. The mate who cannot accept the reality that the relationship has ended will be in denial that it's over and wouldn't know how to take it all in when being told it isn't going to work anymore. In many cases, many men and women become persistent to keep the relationship together, and won't accept that it's over, and forcing someone to love you becomes a problem. No one can force someone to stay into a relationship, and there are some people who just don't get it. This type of situation will call for an intervention from a family member or a trusted friend. Working towards moving on isn't a choice for someone who doesn't get it at first. Staying away and avoiding any communication will help in the healing process. Eventually, finding someone to fall in love with will happen instead of forcing your love on someone who doesn't love you.

You Must Have Dating Rules

A thirty-five year old woman by the name of Samantha said to her friend Delia over the phone, "There's a new man moving in, Delia, you should see him. I've been living in Milton for years and there hasn't been a man living in this three family building the whole time I've been here. He seems to be the new neighbor. I've been watching him move in throughout the day, and after I heard a truck in front of the building. I ran to the window to look out and see what was going on."

Delia replied, "I know you're not seeing anyone right now, but you need to take things slowly. He is going to see you looking out of the window."

"But he is attractive and I'm going to see him often coming and going," Samantha argued.

"Let's be realistic; looking the other way is the right thing to do. I think that you should keep in mind that you need dating rules because you have to live there," Delia explained.

"I know he is living in the same building; I just thought that I could ask him if he was seeing anyone. If he is, then I'll look the other way but if he isn't, then I'm going to ask him out," Samantha decided.

"Think before you start dating a man who lives too close to you. No matter where you're living or working, figure out how to stay away from men living close to you because you have to constantly see him. Try to consider if it's the right choice you're making. I'm your friend Samantha, and I don't want you to cause a problem that could've been avoided. Go elsewhere to find a man to date; it will be easier for you. On the other hand, you may feel uncomfortable and awkward, also there is a possibility if you get involved, it wouldn't last very long. There are rules everywhere we go, such as school and work, so why not have rules when dating? Nothing is wrong with having small talk, but speak to him at a distance when you see him coming and going. Then he will always be respectful because you stayed away. For example, if you know he is home for an intimate encounter. There's a possibility that the man will move out if there isn't a commitment. If he seems to be interested, say respectfully 'No thanks I'm already with someone.' Just try to remember your rules when you want a man who lives extremely close to you. Live

by it and you'll be happier without dealing with the awkwardness if it doesn't work. I think everyone should have some limitations because things can become complicated. For example, he can be a jealous person who might watch you, and will not want to see you with another man in front of the building. So not getting involved
 with your neighbor make sense. Ultimately, try your best to stay at a distance when you see him going in and out of the building."

    Reluctantly, Samantha replied, "I think your right but I'm an adult. I think that I'm going to give him a chance anyway. I can handle whatever comes my way. I know your concern and I know you've dealt with your own personal experiences, but thanks for your advice."

Your Mate Isn't Affectionate Anymore

Many couples desire the touch of their mate on a daily basis. As time passes, being affectionate isn't going to be the same as it once was, if some couples do not find that it's important in a relationship. This is a subject that many couples argue about when looking for attention. Especially, after being overly affectionate at the beginning of the relationship. It's a desire that has to come naturally with your mate, because it can easily be lost as the relationship progresses. It's a good idea to engage in having a pleasant kiss in the morning, after work, or before bedtime. It shouldn't matter who is the one to initiate affection first. If a couple doesn't show they care for each other often, the issue could become disappointing in time. The complaint will be 'Why aren't you affectionate anymore? I thought you loved me?' Then it's time to talk about where the relationship is going. Showing affection towards your mate is wonderful, and it's crucial for a relationship. Doing so is a part of keeping a relationship together long-term.

Ingram Content Group UK Ltd.
Milton Keynes UK
UKHW052140310523
422674UK00004B/54